Window-box Allotment

Frances Lincoln Limited
4 Torriano Mews
Torriano Avenue
London NW5 2RZ
www.franceslincoln.com

First published by Ebury Press 2001
This revised, expanded and illustrated
edition first published by
Frances Lincoln Limited 2012

A catalogue record for this book
is available from the British Library.

9-780-7112-3173-3

Designed by Maria Charalambous
Printed and bound in China

For my Mother,
and the Encouragers,
with love:
Mary Barnard
Richard Brown
Shane Butler
Jo Christian, my publisher
Helen MacTaggart
Almaki Marianos
Eva Papastratis, my literary agent
at Curtis Brown
Kate and Anthony Rogers
Carolina Rawlings
John and Judy Russell
Ann Schlee
and the Tuesday friends

Contents

Introduction

'He who plants a garden plants happiness.'
Chinese proverb

Window-boxes make excellent homes for vegetables, herbs and fruit

Window-boxes don't insist on being planted with petunias, geraniums and dusty rags of trailing ivy. They make equally good homes for vegetables, fruit, spice and herbs. Growing now, in January, in window-boxes, pots and hanging baskets on my west-facing, 16 x 9ft (4.9 x 2.7m) central London roof garden are Swiss chard, frizzy endive, pak choi, perpetual spinach, lamb's lettuce, garlic chives, rocket, mitsuba (a type of Japanese parsley), celeriac, winter purslane and curly-leaf parsley. There will be more later in the year, such as dwarf beans, wild strawberries, tomatoes, 'Salad Bowl' lettuce and aubergines. Most of the vegetables growing now were sown last spring and autumn, except for the spinach and Swiss chard which were sown two years ago.

Containers are perfect for the elderly, children and the disabled

Almost everyone can have a miniature allotment. Young, small hands and elderly, stiff hands can dig or trowel-dig compost that is only a few inches deep. For those who

cannot see, window-boxes and pots are easy for fingers to 'walk' over and examine. They are also good for backs that cannot bend; for those who find sitting (especially in a wheelchair) easier; and for those who prefer kneeling or standing. And for people who live in flats without window ledges, there is seed sprouting to try (see page 143). Only a small investment is needed – hardly an overdraft – and this can be made month by month.

Small-scale container gardening is easier to observe

Both people without and people with gardens can enjoy window-box gardening because it is quite different from 'garden gardening'. Unless you are a snail or a worm, you can't see seeds sprouting: the eyes are too far away from the ground. But containers can be placed at eye level and are on a small scale. Because such gardening is intimate, you are more a part of it and can observe more of what is going on, particularly through a magnifying glass: the cucumber slowly fattening and lengthening, the wild strawberry flower mysteriously changing into fruit. Although it is small, the enjoyment, interest and enrichment it produces are immense.

I am not a horticulturist, just an enthusiastic beginner. What follows are not intended to be dictatorial instructions, but simply suggestions which may be followed, partly followed or ignored.

January

Now is the time for preparation

Start collecting small mustard-and-cress-sized plastic supermarket containers (measuring about 6 x 4 x 2in/15 x 10 x 5cm), preferably transparent ones, because lengthening roots are interesting to watch. Larger containers – those in which the concrete-like supermarket peaches are sold – can also be useful for more vigorous seeds and beans. Also collect the cardboard cores of toilet rolls. These make good cylinders for runner bean germination.

Buy some organic peat-free, seed-sowing compost. As you will be not only admiring the results of your sowing but eating them too, buy organic compost unless you find the idea of garnishing your food with sprinklings of artificial fertilizers appealing. Only a little is needed, so begin with the best.

Organic
The *Oxford English Dictionary* definition:
'Of, relating to, or derived from living matter.
A fertilizer or manure produced from natural substances,
usually without the addition of chemicals.'

One knows these words as acquaintances; the definitions just deepen the acquaintance.

Buy a small sieve for sifting soil; also some plastic plant labels and a soft lead pencil. Invest in the smallest electric propagator. Alternatively, if you're uncertain whether you're going to enjoy window-box gardening, buy a full-sized seed tray with a transparent plastic lid, or a roll of cling film. To prevent the spread of disease, everything should first be washed in a mild solution of household bleach or sterilizing solution and then thoroughly rinsed. This is pleasurable winter-hibernation work, one's hands in warm, soapy water. It makes January a friendlier month and brings spring forward. All that is needed now is time to study the seed catalogues.

Fear of sowing

It is astonishing how many grown-up people have never sown a single seed. The idea of seed sowing seems to fill them with trepidation, as though it is some magical process (which, of course, it is) only for the cognoscenti, and from which they are excluded. In fact seed sowing is one of the simplest things to do. If birds and breezes can do it, it should not be beyond humans, and 75 per cent of the work is done by the seeds themselves.

Trial parsley-seed sowing

For those who have never done any sowing, January is a good time to practise, before the real seed-sowing months arrive. Despite the saying that parsley should be sown when naked by moonlight, it can also be sown successfully indoors, when you are fully clothed and during daylight. It is one of the few plants that can be germinated indoors all the year round.

It is not necessary to have a potting shed, greenhouse or anywhere special to sow seeds. All that is needed is a table spread with newspaper.

The following basic instructions apply to sowing most of the seeds mentioned in this book.

1. Make drainage holes in the bottom of one of the plastic supermarket containers (some are already pierced), piercing them

from the inside out to make certain the drainage works.

2. Crumble any lumps in the compost, then sieve it into the container until it overflows. The compost needs to be fine and friable (easily crumbled) to create a comfortable bed for the seeds and their roots to grow in – imagine yourself living in the compost. For those who are fond of their hands and don't like the idea of touching compost, rub them with barrier cream before resorting to gloves; this at least lets the hands feel what they are touching, whereas gloves do not, a large proportion of the pleasure being on the other side of the glove – one might as well wear gloves while making love.
3. Give the container a firm shake. Level the surface of the compost with something straight, such as a ruler.
4. Gently press the compost down with your palm. Seeds need something firmish, but not rock hard, to rest on.
5. Put the filled container into the sink, then fill the sink with water until it comes halfway up the container's sides. Leave until the compost has drunk its fill and glistens on top like coal. Remove and allow to drain. Watering before sowing avoids disturbing the seeds and makes their sowing simpler, as they are more visible against the water-darkened compost. It also makes it easier to see how much soil to sieve on top. (Another advantage of pot and window-box gardening is that a single packet of seeds can last for several years. Parsley seeds given to me five years ago are still germinating. Seeds of an Arctic lupin have been known to grow after lying in the ground for 10,000 years.)
6. A 6 x 4 x 2in (15 x 10 x 5cm) container will take only about fifteen nasturtium-sized seeds, or fewer. Some seeds, such as Virginia stock (a few flowers have been included for the sake of their scent or colour), prefer to be sown on the surface of the compost and left uncovered. Others need more privacy and require a light covering of soil. The seed packet instructions usually indicate the seeds' needs.
7. Italian plain-leaved parsley seeds are greyish and rowing boat shaped. Mark out five evenly spaced rows of three seeds each by making shallow fingertip indentations in the compost. Place a seed in each hollow. Sieve ⅛in (3mm) of soil over the surface, until the damp compost below disappears. Gently firm the surface with your

palm – just a reassuring pat, the sort you would give to a nervous cat. Remember the shoots have to push their way up through the surface, so don't want too much of a struggle.

8. Write the date, name and number of seeds sown on a label, stick this into the edge of the container.
9. Cover the container with a plastic lid or some cling film, or put it into the electric propagator. When using a propagator, first spray its base (on which a little compost or sand has been laid) with water, as this helps to create a Turkish bath-like atmosphere. Place on a semi-sunny bedroom windowsill where it will be checked at least twice a day and won't suffer from neglect.
10. After a short time the walls and ceiling of the propagator or container cover will start to warm and pour with sweat. The tiny glow-worm light of a propagator-incubator switches itself on and off. Whether it is wishful thinking or just imagination, the bedroom feels different. There is a sense (particularly during the night) of something else being in the room other than a human being. Even though the seeds are only minuscule in size, they are alive. You are not alone.

Types of parsley

The world of parsley is more mysterious than one might think. I am advised by an expert that flat-leaved parsley (*Petroselinum crispum* var. *neapolitanum*) includes French, Italian and Neapolitan sorts such as 'Gigante di Napoli' (commonly known as 'Italian Giant'. There are also moss-curled sorts (*Petroselinum crispum*) such as 'Champion' and 'Rina', and Hamburg (root) parsley. Japanese parsley (mitsuba, *Cryptotaenia*) is closely related. All have a different taste, appearance, colour and texture. Why not become a parsley specialist?

Or, if you don't like parsley or are anxious about sowing seeds, you could, if you have a cat, grow a portable cat-grass 'lawn'. These can be found (pre-sown) in boxes in pet shops and some supermarkets. Just add water. Each morning, my cat rushes like a health fanatic to her portable lawn and, head tilted sideways, chews down the stems, enjoying a pre-breakfast salad.

More things to do in January

Go to the public library, children's section, and look for a book on seeds to find out what is inside those grey rowing-boat-shaped parsley seeds. Children's books are, on the whole, better illustrated than adults' and, on subjects like this, easier to understand. Within the seed coat lies a minuscule seed (the ovule of a plant), inside which is a tiny new plant, consisting of a seed leaf, shoot and root (and a larder of food to live on).

Find out about wormeries, although it is still too cold to inaugurate one yet (see page 20).

Plan on starting a simple compost heap in a plastic sack or plastic dustbin (see page 39).

Look out for unusual vegetables in greengrocers and supermarkets. Go to Chinese, Caribbean, Turkish and Indian greengrocers and buy vegetables you have never seen before and whose names you don't know. Choose those that have root-sprouting possibilities. Chinese single-clove garlic, lemongrass, sweet potatoes, Japanese artichokes: all these, and more, can be started off indoors in water or suspended just above it, the base touching but not submerged (or else it will rot). In the case of sweet potatoes, if one end doesn't root, turn it upside down and try the other.

If possible, buy organic seeds (see page 170) to stop the spread of non-germinating, terminator-gene seeds. These are sterile seeds – unlike the fertile profits of some seed companies, which force us to buy more and more seeds instead of saving them. Terminator-gene seeds must be one of the most dire combinations of mammonism and immorality – something that one imagines could only take place in science fiction.

The days are getting lighter by a minute a day, or so says *The Times*. The lid of darkness is being raised, fractionally, and with it our expectation. The following is a sample from a seed-sowing diary I wrote last spring when growing tomatoes for the first time:

Seed sowing diary

Day 1 A packet of tomato seeds: so light in weight there's no castanet rattle when they are shaken. Yet these dust-sized specks (assisted by the four elements) contain potential stems, scent, leaves, pollen, colour, root and rootlets, taste, flesh, sap, flowers, texture, fruit, juice and yet more seeds for next year's harvest: they contain the future – something that should never be taken for granted. An electric propagator: it is attached by a cord to a plug, has a greenhouse-like top with ventilation slides and fits on a bedroom windowsill. Compost: moist, warmish in its plastic sack and fine; I would be perfectly content to germinate in this comfortable-looking soil. Sift it through your fingers like making short-crust pastry. The seed tray is filled to the brim, levelled, then firmed down with a presser board, which resembles a wooden palm on the surface of the soil. A pinch of the fragile, fly-away seeds is scattered from above. If two or more seeds insist on lying together, coax them apart – a fingertip away from each other. Between the palms, a 'rain' of ¼ in (6mm) of compost is sifted, then gently pressed down. (Or sift it through the small plastic sieve.) Greenhouse cover is placed on top, 'electric blanket' switched on, propagator put on the windowsill and the curtain a quarter drawn to shade the tray from too much light. This compost bed has been made with more care than one makes one's own. After sowing, the invisible seeds are left alone in their centrally heated indoor 'greenhouse'. It is time to wait. Wake up in the night to see if tiny orange thermostat light is on. Wonder what is silently and mysteriously taking place in the soil – or perhaps not so silently if one could really hear: the sound of seed cases preparing to split open.

Day 2, a.m. Greenhouse top is misted and sweating. Peer through the misting to see if anything is happening. It isn't – visibly.

Day 5, early morning Faint eruptions have appeared on the soil surface; they could have been made by tentative moles.

Day 5, later in the day Mole eruptions have become larger and are now miniature earthquakes, as the thin-as-hair stems push upwards, heads still buried.

Day 5, evening Heads are still buried, arched stems resembling croquet hoops on lawn.

Day 5, midnight Croquet hoops are no longer there. In only a few hours the heads have risen, breaking out of their seed coats, and are now upright, two-leaved. What force is needed, first, to create the upheavals in the compost and, second, to raise the fragile stems from horizontal to vertical?

Day 6, 6 a.m. Remove greenhouse top. Seedlings lean away from the room towards the window, leaves outstretched horizontally like a troupe of gymnasts.

Day 6, 9 p.m. Leaves raised upwards, folded together: gymnasts exercising.

Day 7, morning Turn tray round so that leaning-towards-the-light seedlings can straighten their stems.

Day 7, evening All stems are straight. After a few more windowsill days in the sun with the curtain protecting them at night from the open window's air, it is time for them to go outside. First into a miniature outdoor 'greenhouse' (i.e. a large plastic cloche), but only for the choicest slice of the day – its middle. Then back they come in the late afternoon.

In and out they go each morning and evening. All of the seed packet's promised contents have germinated. All thirty stems are now protected by the finest, fur-like hairs – vertical haloes when seen against the light. Only a few are late beginners, handicapped by seed cases that remain clamped to their two leaves, preventing them from opening. It is tempting to assist and release them, but more interesting to resist and see how the struggling leaves manage to free themselves.

It is time to do a little judicious thinning-out of seedlings that are growing too close together, endangering each other. Now's the moment to test whether they already smell or taste of tomato. They don't, neither stem nor leaves. But then the shape of the first two seed leaves gives no hint of what they are going to become – unlike basil at the same age. Long before basil seedlings are 'large enough to handle', they are imbued with the clove-ish spiciness of their future.

Day 11 Third leaf is preparing to appear. It is triple-, not single-lobed, even in infancy, and this is the first sign of the tomato plant it is going to become. Does this visual indication also hold the identifying smell and taste? No. Still it releases no scent or taste.

Day 12 Although the tomato plants are still too fragile to be watered from above, even with a fine rose spray, they are now sturdy enough to stand up for themselves against breezes, trembling only slightly without toppling over. Watering is done with the narrowest watering-can spout, dribbled on to the compost in which desert-like cracks appear.

Seed sowing must be one of the most absorbing of occupations. It is not only the actual doing of it, but also the anticipation, the anxieties and thoughts surrounding it . . . imagining what is going on *inside* the seed tray, as the white galaxy of fragile roots spreads through the dark earth.

Day 12, 10 p.m. Rush back early from a party to close the window and rescue the tomato plants from an unexpected drop in temperature.

Day 18 Pricking-out day – the move from tray to individual pots. Fill 3½in (9cm) pots with compost. Use both thumbs to make a hole in the centre – like making a clay pinch-pot – to receive the plant and its roots. Scoop out a heaped dessertspoonful of chocolate-coloured cake compost, in the centre of which is a small, giraffe-like creature with its long, furry-neck stem and white spider's-web roots. Place in the hole.

One by one the pots line up. Glance down and notice that the first of the transplants is drooping; prop it up with a pea-size piece of compost. Only a few minutes later, in the time it took to make a cup of coffee, panic! Fifteen plants are drooping – sulking in unison. Race at ambulance speed to place the fifteen casualties ankle-deep in a trough of water.

Wait for the first signs of recovery and discover the compost bag's planting instructions: the pots should have been watered before, not after, pricking out. It is touch and go. After what seems a long time, but is in fact short, for stems and leaves to rise from facing the earth to facing the sky, the panic is over.

First whole night in 'greenhouse'.

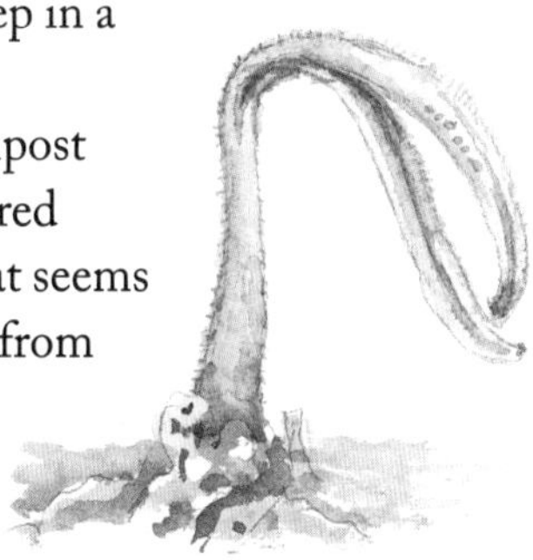

Day 19 Raise cloche to see how plants have fared in their pots. All are flourishing.

Day 22 Fifth leaf appearing. Plants are now stocky enough to be watered from above with a fine rose spray. Stems are thickening. Fur-like stem hairs stop at the two first leaves; then the fur thins out, becoming like fine barbed wire, to deter insects perhaps.

Day 25 Three-lobed leaves are now sufficiently resilient for raindrops to balance and perch on them without toppling them. When twenty-nine plants are flourishing with four or five leaves, the last of the late beginners' first two leaves still remain clasped together, forcing the growing tip sideways; despite this stubbornness, the third and fourth leaves have managed to open. At last, by bending low over the tomato plants, it is possible to smell the peppery scent that they keep so close to themselves. Soon gangly adolescent stems will need cane supports. The rest of the tomato story is known.

Liked and disliked tomatoes

'Gardener's Delight' tomatoes have such a specific taste and are so sweet, small and juicy they are more like fruits (their original definition) than vegetables. On the other hand, 'Marmande' tomatoes resemble sumo wrestlers (in size, approximately six 'Gardener's Delight' equal one 'Marmande'). They have an unappealing, half-asleep taste of pink water and an unpleasant soft texture which offers about as much resistance as damp cotton wool. When they are grown in their country of origin perhaps they are different.

Purple potato harvest

5 January. From a 9in (23cm) deep x 8in (20cm) wide pot I am 'digging' up a harvest of new potatoes. The 'digging' is being done with my hands, which

is far more enjoyable than using a trowel or fork. When my fingers are buried in the compost, they feel blindfolded as they sift their way through the soil, searching for solid shapes as though playing hide and seek. Is this how worms (which have no eyes) feel when travelling through the earth? It reminds me of being in one of those 'black' restaurants where one eats in pitch darkness.

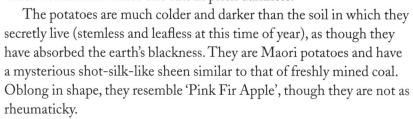

The potatoes are much colder and darker than the soil in which they secretly live (stemless and leafless at this time of year), as though they have absorbed the earth's blackness. They are Maori potatoes and have a mysterious shot-silk-like sheen similar to that of freshly mined coal. Oblong in shape, they resemble 'Pink Fir Apple', though they are not as rheumaticky.

After rinsing them (they hardly need washing and the sooner they are placed in boiling water or a steamer, the better) you will discover that the blackness is in fact a somber Lenten purple. When they are cut in two the purple lightens, though it is still purple – there is nothing lilacy about it; but the flesh is slightly marbled. If a potato is placed on your palm, it leaves a purple imprint and reveals, surprisingly, how sappy and juicy potatoes can be. When placed in a pot of bubbling water, the potatoes resemble hippos wallowing in a blue-green spa.

Unlike some purple or blackish potatoes, these retain their colour when cooked. Their texture is dense and the taste slightly chestnutty, not really in need of either salt or butter. It is the only purple food I have eaten, the colour giving it a rather serious taste. (One can now buy purple potatoes in England, but not Maori potatoes.)

These Maori potatoes lead a somewhat complicated life: Maori in name, South American in origin, papal purple in colour, and requiring to be planted on Good Friday. Obviously an Antipodean Easter is the opposite of our northern hemisphere variety: considering all this confusion, it is astonishing that they flourish at all, but they do.

These potatoes were planted in mid-April a year ago. Despite their complicated ancestry it did not take them all this time to decide to grow, so this was not their first harvest. I keep them in the soil instead of in a larder or refrigerator.

Wildlife trials

Apart from my roof garden, I have a very small shady garden in which almost nothing grows, willingly. It has been sown with wild flowers but instead of the poppy, cornflower and daisy tapestry I imagined, all that emerged were spindly weeds. Next came strawberries, wild and tame. Although they produced flowers, they obviously decided that that was enough. I then tried potatoes, assuming that as most of their growing is done underground in pitch darkness, they wouldn't be too fussy about shade. Although they produced promising haulm bouquets, the crop consisted of a few marble-sized potatoes which, when cooked, were indistinguishable from pebbles. The final attempt was an asparagus bed. This involved waiting in anticipation for a year before the first spears appeared. When they, the two of them, did appear they were toothpick thin. The only plant which grows enthusiastically is minute, bright green and resembles bouclé knitting.

I then made a grandiose decision: I would relinquish the whole plot – as though it was at least Sissinghurst – and dedicate it to wildlife conservation. I studied catalogues: there would be a bat box, bumblebee nester, ladybird feeder, frog cabin, pond, nest boxes and a hedgehog bungalow. Hedgehog rescue centres, I had been informed, were in need of additional accommodation for elderly and disabled residents.

Before ordering, I did some research. The first disappointment was the bat box. Although I have seen bats scything through the air only feet away from my flat, apparently it faces in the wrong direction for their shelters. As I am not prepared to move, that was that. I ordered a 'sparrow terrace', what resembled a crotched 'nest pocket' for wrens, an 'easy clean' blue tit box and a tawny owl nest tube. Before ordering the frogs' pond ramp, I discovered that ponds need sunshine to prevent them from stagnating. Also, as the garden is walled, it is unlikely that any homeless frog would leapfrog over the 7-ft/2m wall on the off chance that there might be a pond plus vacant accommodation on the other side. Although the ladybird chalet looks attractive, there probably would not be much to observe. The same applies to the solitary bee nester. This is a log drilled with masses of holes resembling one-room flats, presumably used for resting and nesting, so would hardly be a hive of activity.

The most disappointing result of the research was that my desirable little garden proved to be unsuitable as a hedgehog sanctuary.

'Hedgies', I was informed, 'need a lawn and a two-mile run when foraging for food.'

'Even disabled or elderly hedgies?' I enquired, feeling over-familiar using the diminutive.

'Yes.' (To create the illusion of space, some people buy treadmills for their hedgehogs, but I don't care for the idea of any creature endlessly walking nowhere.)

'What about visually impaired hedgehogs?' I asked, careful to avoid the word 'blind'. 'And how' – I felt slightly guilty persisting – 'would they know? Wouldn't they assume that the bouclé knitting was a lawn?'

'Many hedgies are quite disorientated already.' Was this a euphemism for Alzheimer's? Apart from a bungalow, which has an internal corridor (nice enough to move into oneself), I imagined that their only other need would be the occasional saucer of milk.

'When they've stopped hibernating, they need feeding.' This meant that only during hibernation (the worst of the winter months) would I be able to go away.

The last possibility was a solar insect theatre. Its light switches on automatically at dusk, enticing lacewings, moths, butterflies and other thespians through its side panels, i.e. the stage equivalent of 'wings'. Included was an insect 'landing perch'.

Immediately it arrived I prepared the prescribed sugar/water attractant and waited in anticipation for dusk, as though waiting for a first night. Not even a clothes moth condescended to make a debut. After a few days the attractant evaporated. The next item on the menu was dark beer heated with molasses and brown sugar. Result: hardly a sell-out at either the matinée or evening performance. The third attractant was over-ripe banana mashed with rum. Result: the theatre remained empty, and I was left with a bunch of black

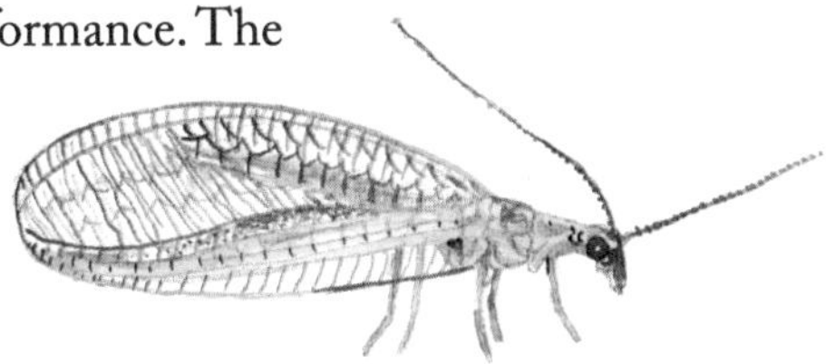

bananas (something I particularly dislike) and almost full bottles of dark beer and brandy plus a tin of molasses – not the easiest of ingredients to amalgamate into one's diet.

Four months later: not even a fly has landed on the insect perch. Apart from one short 'let', the nest boxes have remained vacant, making me feel like a failed estate agent.

Seeds to sow now, indoors

Italian flat-leaved parsley (*Petroselinum crispum* var. *neapolitanum*)
'Gardener's Delight' tomatoes (*Solanum lycopersicum*) (January–March, says the packet)
Sweet peas (*Lathyrus odoratus*) (January–mid-May)

WHAT TO EAT NOW

Fried parsley: an alternative to croutons

Why did fried parsley become unfashionable, to be replaced by fried seaweed, which is generally not seaweed but cabbage?

2 large handfuls of parsley

corn oil (or other mild-flavoured oil)

Remove the lower, thicker stems from two large handfuls of what is now imaginatively called 'bunched parsley' (i.e. 'Champion' moss-curled parsley). Wash thoroughly. Drain and dry even more thoroughly. In a wok heat about half an inch of corn oil until very hot. When a test piece of parsley sizzles and rises to the top when placed in the oil, put the rest in. Fry until crisp and dark green. Remove with a slotted spoon and drain on several sheets of absorbent paper.

February

A riddle

Question: What creature has no eyes, ears, nose, teeth,
arms or legs? Yet this creature has five hearts; it moves, eats,
breathes through its skin, has senses, is both male and female,
mates – with both males and females – can live for fifteen years
or longer, never sleeps. And makes new earth.
Answer: An earthworm.

With their constant munching and mating, breeding, producing of vermicompost and lack of sleep, what exhausting lives worms live!

There are not a lot of gardening activities at this time of the year, so now would be a good moment to consider making or buying a wormery and producing worm casts, i.e. worm manure.

'When we behold a wide, turf-covered expanse, we would remember that its smoothness, on which so much of its beauty depends, is mainly due to all the inequalities having been slowly levelled by worms. It is a marvellous reflection that the whole of the superficial mould over any such expanse has passed, and will again pass every few years, through the bodies of worms. It may be doubted whether there are many other animals which have played so important a role in the history of the world as these lowly organized creatures.'

Charles Darwin (1809–82)

The Earthworm

Who really respects the earthworm,
the farmworker far under the grass in the soil.
He keeps the earth always changing.
He works entirely full of soil,
speechless with soil, and blind.
He is the underneath farmer, the underground one,
where the fields are getting on their harvest clothes.
Who really respects him,
this deep and calm earth-worker,
this deathless, grey, tiny farmer in the planet's soil.

Harry Edmund Martinson
From the Swedish (trans. Robert Bly)

Windowsill wormeries

Wormeries are ideal for window-box gardens: a) because they are small, b) because they can, if necessary, be kept indoors, c) because the worms require only small amounts of food, and d) because a working wormery is most interesting to watch.

Some people can't even bear to hear the word 'worm' said aloud, let alone whispered. But after reading about the intriguing life of worms and being introduced to them gradually – perhaps to a baby worm first, and then to the head end of an adolescent – even the most squeamish might overcome their aversion. It is worth it.

Worms have enthusiastic appetites and eat their way through half their own body weight in food each day. Because they have special digestive systems, the results of their banqueting, worm casts (the earth that is excreted by worms), are much richer in nutrients than the original food. Worm-cast compost can be mixed with existing soil when refreshing window-boxes in the spring (see page 42), used as a slow-release top dressing or as an alternative to peat. (If, when in Ireland, you have ever seen peat being machine dug from the body of the land, you will probably never use it again.)

You can make your own wooden wormery (both Garden Organic and Chase Organics provide instructions – see page 170). Or you can buy one or enquire whether your local council will give you one free (or at a reduced rate), this being the council's attempt to encourage people to recycle and cut down on the landfill-waste problem. This is an excellent initiative but has its drawbacks: I have tried two council plastic wormeries and neither worked, the result in both cases being a swamp at the bottom of the bins from which the worms, quite understandably, were constantly trying to escape. I also bought what appeared to be an airier version of the council's wormery. Result: third swamp. Conclusion: worms don't like living in airless plastic containers. Who would? I have yet to meet a worm composter who has had any success with plastic – or at least with this particular design. I am sorry for those people who have given up worm composting because of failure, because wormeries *can* work.

The most successful wormery I have had was called a Tiger Worm Compost Bin and was made of recycled newspapers and cardboard (see page 170, E). It allowed air to enter and excess moisture to leave and evaporate. Owing to its composition, it won't last for ever, though mine lasted for several years. At the moment I am experimenting with what might, or might not, turn out to be the simplest and cheapest design of all (see page 104).

In the meantime, while making your own wormery or waiting for an ordered one to arrive, here are a few worm 'biographical' details.

The species generally used for vermicomposting are the red worm (*Eisenia andrei*) and the tiger worm (*E. fetida*), so called because of its dark reddish colour and buff stripes. The reds and tigers are not from the same family as common earthworms (*Lumbricus terrestris*), which live deeper down in the earth and do different work, burrowing and aerating the soil. Reds and tigers live in the organic mulch on the earth's surface and spend most of their time eating and producing nutrients for the soil. Without worms there would be no plants or trees.

'Earthworms are the intestines of the earth.'
Aristotle (381–322 BC)

Worm myth: one of the questions frequently asked about worms is: if they are cut in two, do they grow another head and rear? No. This is just one of those stories we like and seem to need to keep, but is as far from the truth as the story about bats being blind and having a fondness for entangling themselves in people's hair. However, sometimes the head end of a cut-in-half worm will survive.

First parsley check

By now the results of the trial parsley-seed sowing should be making an appearance. Keep an eye on what is happening beneath the steamy propagator lid, but don't lift and peep too often. This lowers the temperature, reduces the claustrophobic, tropical atmosphere and is intrusive. After a week, more or less (each seed is different), specks of bright greenness will be seen against the dark compost. A day or so later the specks will rise, their fragile stems finer than babies' hair. Some seedlings emerge still 'wearing' their hat-like seed coats. As hour by hour they grow taller, open the propagator vents to let in a little outside-world air.

When the majority have made their debut (another advantage of counting them while sowing), it is time to move them from the intensive care of the propagator-incubator to the less sheltered maternity ward of the windowsill, with its changing temperatures, air currents and direct sunlight. Place the container on top of the propagator lid, where there may be some remnants of warmth.

Studying seed catalogues

Now is a good time to start looking through seed catalogues, a most pleasurable winter-evening-by-lamplight occupation. Just seeing the pictures and reading the descriptions – of sugar snap peas and night-scented stock – makes summer leap out of the February darkness. What is almost unimaginable when sitting in front of a fire on a dark winter's evening – open windows, endless summer days, languorous evenings – suddenly becomes imaginable. Here is a list of vegetables (just some of them), herbs, scented plants and a spice that can be grown in window-boxes and pots:

Abyssinian mustard (also known by the less beguiling name of Texsel greens) – a recently introduced brassica, with glossy leaves and a spinach flavour
Alpine strawberry (*Fragaria vesca* 'Semperflorens')
Aubergine (*Solanum melongena*)
Basil (*Ocimum basilicum*)
Beans, dwarf French (*Phaseolus vulgaris*) and runner (*Phaseolus coccineus*)
Beetroot (*Beta vulgaris*) 'Detroit 2-Tardel'
Chicory (*Cichorium intybus*) – use young leaves for salads
Chinese cabbage (*Brassica rapa* Chinensis Group)
Chives (*Allium schoenoprasum*)
Cress, American land (*Barbarea verna*, also called Belle Isle cress, early winter cress and upland cress) – remains green all winter; can be used instead of watercress
Cucumber (*Cucumis sativa*)
Dill (*Anethum graveolens*)
Garlic (*Allium sativum*)
Garlic chives (*Allium tuberosum*)
Komatsuna (also called mustard spinach) – Japanese, related to the turnip; use in salads or wait a little longer and stir-fry
Lamb's lettuce (*Valerianella locusta*, also called corn salad and mâche)
Lettuce (*Lactuca sativa*), 'Salad Bowl' and 'Black Seeded Simpson'
Mignonette – for its scent
Mitsuba (also called Japanese parsley) – the seeds are slim and dark jade green with vertical stripes; has an angelica taste
Mizuna (also called potherb mustard) – Japanese, juicy – can be cooked or used in salads
Nasturtium (*Tropaeolum majus*)
Night-scented stock (*Matthiola longipetala* subsp. *bicornis*)
Oriental saladini – a mixture of oriental salads
Pak choi – can be eaten as a salad
Parsley (*Petroselinum crispum*)
Peas (*Pisum sativum*), mangetout and sugar snap
Perpetual spinach

Potato (*Solanum tuberosum*)
Radish (*Raphanus sativus*)
Rocket (*Eruca versicaria* subsp. *sativa*)
Saffron (*Crocus sativus*)
Scarole – use in salads
Spinach (*Spinacia oleracea*)
Sweet pepper (*Capsicum annuum* Grossum Group)
Swiss chard (*Beta vulgaris* Cicla Group)
Tomato (*Solanum lycopersicum*)
Vegetable amaranth – use in salads or stir-fries
Winter purslane (also called miner's lettuce, Indian lettuce, claytonia); has heart-shaped succulent leaves; use in salads.

Window-box gardening is more suited, on the whole, to cut-and-come-again vegetables, such as 'Salad Bowl' lettuce, Swiss chard and perpetual spinach, which continually replenish themselves throughout their growing season. A single 'Tom Thumb' lettuce is cut once, and that's that until the next one is sown.

Resist the temptation to buy too many plants or seeds. They all need attention, but not fragmented or diluted attention, under which they will not thrive – and neither will the sower. Growing seeds is like travelling, in that it is better to see more of less, than less of more. Your concentration acts like a fertilizer – just as it does on both humans and animals. If you stroke a person or an animal while reading or listening to the radio, your hand feels empty and automatic. Animals are particularly aware of this and, quite rightly, object. You have to remember what you are doing when sowing seeds: you are helping to perform a miracle. That something the size of a speck of dust, which can be blown away by a breeze, sneeze or sigh, needs only to be placed in or on soil to germinate is miraculous. There are vegetables to match the whole spectrum of colour, apart from blue. So why is blue mostly excluded, reserved for flowers and sky?

And how undemanding vegetables are. They will flourish in fields, suspended in mid-air in hanging baskets, in greenhouses, pots, pans, allotments, potagers, roof gardens and terraces.

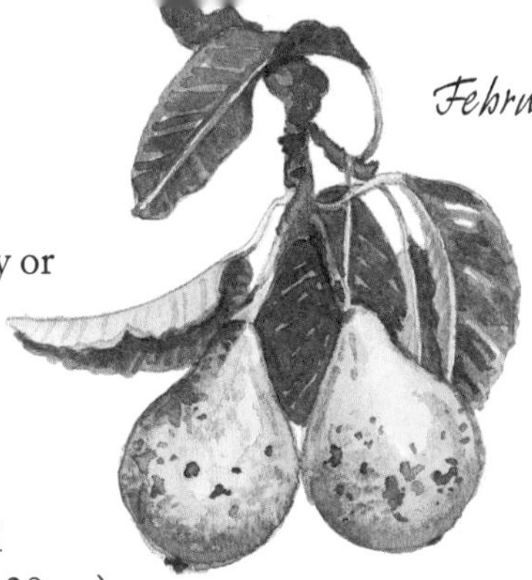

Planning an orchard

Even if you have only a very small, sunny balcony or roof garden there is still room to include an orchard, or at least one miniature, self-fertile fruit tree (see page 170, F). My roof garden started off with a 'Comice' and a 'Conference' pear, a 'Victoria' plum and a 'Sunburst' cherry, all comfortably growing in 14 x 14 x 12in (36 x 36 x 30cm) tubs. At least they are sufficiently comfortable to produce fruit.

Now is the moment to order an 'orchard'. Trees can be planted between November and April and generally arrive with simple planting instructions.

Confession number one: an orchard

Any number of fruit trees beyond three constitutes, for me, that evocative word, an orchard. Mine consists of three 'Victoria' plums, one 'Brown Turkey' fig, a 'Sunburst' cherry, a 'Comice' and a 'Conference' pear and a nameless now-no-longer-with-us apple tree. All are of the minarette kind and all, apart from the apple, are of that somewhat solitary, self-sufficient disposition, self-fertile.

There is only one drawback to an orchard, as far as I am concerned, and that is the problem of pruning. For some reason I seem incapable of comprehending even the simplest, most basic pruning instructions, even when lavishly illustrated. The confession: I ring the nursery which supplies my trees and with a cordless telephone held firmly between shoulder and ear, and secateurs at the ready, ask to speak to a patient assistant, who then instructs while I snip. So far this has always worked.

One of the loveliest aspects of an orchard is the spring blossom, each variety of fruit having a different flower. The apple, not being self-fertile, needed a little assistance with fertilizing. This was achieved by gently dabbing the centre of the blossom with a small soft paintbrush.

Pruning the fig tree had a rather biblical feel about it. The large, five-lobed, hand-shaped rough leaves and mysterious thick white sap made me feel I was in the Garden of Eden taking part in Genesis.

Ordering saffron corms

Mid-February is also the time to order saffron (*Crocus sativus*) corms (see page 170, G) for planting between June and August. It is important to buy *C. sativus* and not a subspecies or *C. speciosus*, which is what a lot of the so-called *C. sativus* corms are.

Read about saffron's long and interesting history (for a potted version a a description of a visit to a Spanish saffron festival, see page 109).

Chitting potatoes

This means placing potatoes in an egg box and leaving them in a cool plac to start sprouting (chitting) in time for planting in April.

Second parsley check

After only a few hours on the windowsill, the seedling stems will have straightened. When the sun reaches them, all members of the ensemble w lean towards it. Keep turning their tray clockwise (clockwise because it is easier to remember), so that all sides receive equal light. If seedlings respo in this way to the sun, do they respond nocturnally, too, to the moon? Som gardeners believe so and sow at night. If the moon changes people's mood and pulls tides along, surely it influences seeds, too, pulling them out of their cases.

Scented plants

Although my 'allotment' consists mainly of vegetables and fruit, it was formerly a scented roof garden, so naturally there are still a few members of the scented congregation left, such as Persian lilac, *Wisteria sinensis*, vanilla-scented *Clematis montana*, *Rosa* 'Zéphirine Drouhin', freesias, a portable indoor-outdoor orange bush, *Viburnum* x *burkwoodii*, lavender and *Lilium regale*, which have been living contentedly in the same 8in (20cm) pots for many years. There are also three different honeysuckles, two jasmines and *Trachelospermum* x *jasminoides* 'Japonicum', which specializes in autumns, having two each year – the first a private one in spring, when the leaves turn bright red,

and the second with all the other plants in autumn, when the leaves again become red.

Apart from the residents mentioned above, night-scented stock (which must be one of the smallest flowers to produce such a huge scent) can also be grown. It doesn't object to being brought indoors for the evening to scent a room. Also sweet peas and mignonette, that old-fashioned-looking, grandmotherly plant. If a choice had to be made between vegetables, fruit, scented plants and plants for colour, I would put them in the above order.

For brilliance and cheerfulness there is the confetti-like Virginia stock, nasturtiums and impatiens, the last because of their clashing pink-reds and because they are supposed to be difficult to grow (or at least the F_1 hybrid is). Their germination boosts horticultural confidence.

However, growing solely vegetables need not result in a colourless, flowerless garden. There are red and white bean flowers, yellow cucumber, purple aubergine, beige rocket, pale yellow pak choi and white basil flowers, to mention just a few.

Third parsley check

After a short time the first two seedling leaves will unclasp each other and stretch out horizontally. When they are all outstretched, there will be very little standing room in the seed tray. Possibly a few other seeds (generally known as weeds) will also have enjoyed the incubation period. Remove them and any weak or overcrowded parsley seedlings. This can be done either with agile fingertips or tweezers.

Do not discard the parsley seedlings – eat them. These slim, elongated leaves are unidentifiable as parsley (it is the third leaf that reveals what the plant is), except in their taste, which could be nothing else but parsley. It is astonishing that something so diminutive, which is just a few days old and has only a stem and two leaves, can be filled with its own unmistakable taste, many times more pungent than its size but occupying only a minute portion of the mouth.

Germination summary

Sown 28 January
First appearance 6 February
First two leaves 19 February
Third leaf revealed 21 February. This is the tiny, trifoliate leaf that announces what the plant is: not dill, wild strawberry or basil (these look completely different) but Italian flat-leaved parsley.

Observing a dried pea 'hatching'

For several weeks the pea lay submerged in water in a little glass cup, covered in minute diamond-like bubbles. Was the pea releasing air to create these bubbles? Or where do they come from? After a time I thought the pea might rot, so I removed it from the water and placed it on blotting paper.

Pea has rather anaemic-looking beige skin which makes it resemble a stone, giving it an unyielding appearance.

I keep watching it. What, I wonder, is going on inside it? Has pea put on weight?

Finally, while I was looking in the other direction, the stone-like skin relented and split. It wasn't a random, haphazard splitting. It was a neat little incision, as though made by a tailor. As the split widened, it looked as though a size eighteen person was trying to squeeze out of a size fourteen waistcoat.

After few more days, a minute Roman-nose-profiled beak appeared between the split.

Hatching is almost complete.

Bird Café

In the winter, when my cat died and nothing much was happening on my roof garden, I decided to concentrate on feeding wild birds, hoping I would have more success with them than the wildlife garden experiment.

From a wooden washing line – i.e, a broom handle suspended horizontally – I hung a selection of feeders, including a suet ball, a globe distributor for small birds, a fat ball guardian for larger birds, a classic seed feeder and a goldfinch starter kit. To prevent pigeons stealing the ground feeders' food, on the ground I installed a feeding tray plus a protector which resembled a high-sided cot with lid. (My adept pigeons eat from every food source they can reach.)

The menu consisted of sunflower hearts, premium peanuts in a nylon Aertex 'sock', black sunflower seeds for chaffinches, nyjer seeds for siskins and goldfinches, and high-energy suet sprinkles. For a treat there was a peanut bird cake. As far as possible there was something to suit all tastes and sizes of beak and throat. I resisted buying the *Cooking for Birds* book.

Also suspended from the broom handle was a ceramic birdbath-cum-drinking trough. I did not buy the Grecian, neoclassical or terrazzo birdbaths or the pagoda bird table.

The Bird Café was now open. Several weeks passed. Not even a pigeon appeared.

Remembering a friend's enviably successful relationships with a blackbird family, I followed her advice and added cheese, raisins and grapes to the Today's Specials menu. Still no customers.

Only when I had almost given up hope did the first robin appear. Although I was longing for birds to appear, I was glad that my arms were not long enough to pluck them from the air. They came when they, not I, wanted.

The staircase leading to the roof garden was converted into a hide where I sat and watched the birds through binoculars. What other wild creatures bring so much instant, unexpected delight?

Day by day they became braver until one afternoon a blue tit flew triumphantly through my late cat's cat flap, continuing its flight downstairs into the sitting room, where I was afraid it would crash into a window. Instead it landed on a potted stephanotis, which it examined thoroughly before flying out through another window.

A robin hopped to within inches of my outstretched hand, seemingly compelled for some mysterious reason to move closer and closer. A daring ground-feeder pigeon

hung from the suspended feeders resembling a novice circus artist. With admirable perseverance it tried repeatedly to solve the problem of food behind bars.

One day during spring I went to inspect my transplanted vegetable seedlings, all painstakingly reared from seed on my bedroom windowsill before being tucked comfortably into larger pots. The fragile plants had disappeared. Where *were* they? On the ground, wilting. But how had they got there? They couldn't have clambered out of the pots.

Although I didn't need any help with my 8 x 16ft (2.5 x 5m) roof garden, a blackbird had immediately appointed himself assistant gardener. Everything I transplanted he discarded, his beak flinging it and the surrounding soil on to the ground. At first I thought he might be averse to certain plants. This was not the case. Black disliked all small plants. It was like working with a delinquent adolescent gardener on work experience. When I was not trying to rescue the discarded transplants, I was sweeping up after him, our job descriptions reversed, I having become his full-time assistant. How, I marvelled and fumed, can such a tiny, yellow implement and two small feet do so much damage and how can something smaller than my hand contain so much persistence and strength?

To distract Black from his gardening activities I concocted a playpen, which I filled with fresh compost topped with leaves, having been told that blackbirds enjoy delving into them for worms while kicking them up and creating leaf fountains. Needless to say, Black ignored the playpen, just glancing at it sharply over his shoulder before continuing his determined digging. His reaction was similar to my cat's when I bought a toy for her, her expression one of condescension, as though enquiring *who* I imagined was going to play with it.

After completing his clearance work, Black turned to archaeology. With his legs apart and his head lowered in concentration, he plunged his beak yet further into the soil, excavating it. He was assisted by his two fledgling offspring, though there was nothing baby bird-ish about this couple. They were large, untidy and had squeaky voices. It was impossible to imagine they would ever develop into soloists. They stood close together on their spindly legs, absorbed in watching their manic father.

The last straw was when I discovered that the bedroom window-box, which was planted with basil, dwarf beans, dill and tomatoes, had been ransacked, the young giraffe-like dill plants left gasping for soil. I keep the window wide open all summer so that the tomatoes can be plucked from the bed and made into basil and tomato sandwiches. Not only were all the plants wrenched up but soil was spattered over the white duvet. The only solution, I concluded reluctantly, was to cover the containers with plastic netting.

I began by making individual container covers. As this required the skill of a tailor, which I don't possess, I changed the design and made a series of multi-container hairnet-like covers. But even these had to be gathered at the bottom and, using a needle and twine, tied with a bow. Although the hairnets kept some of the birds out, they also kept the plants in, distorting their growth, particularly the raspberries, which struggled against the netting like prison inmates.

There had never been any trouble sharing the roof garden with cats; none of them had ever mistaken the tubs for litter trays. Now I could barely see out of the bedroom window and, covered in this bridal netting veil, the roof garden resembled something designed by Miss Havisham.

A day after installing the 'prison', who was happily digging away on the inside of the high security net but Black? *How* had this Houdini-in-reverse managed to get in? And equally important, how was he going to get out without panicking and injuring himself? To tempt him away from his digging and to compensate for the now-forbidden garden, I made him a Special Menu order of pre-soaked and chopped raisins, waiting until the hot soaking water cooled because he was apt to stomp about in the bowl.

While Black ate the raisins, feeding some of them to his now outsize dishevelled 'babies', I searched for his secret route into the prison. It was then that I discovered some mysterious molehills on the surface of the soil. Had Black progressed from archaeology to constructing cairns? I never saw him working on his new hobby, and it was doubtful that he did it during the night. I flattened the molehills. Mysteriously, the next morning there they were again.

It was at this time that I had planned to go on holiday. At least, I had assumed, with wild birds there wouldn't be the worry there was with cats when leaving them. I filled all the feeders to their brims and left.

On my return the feeders were empty. But where were the birds? Although the garden was bursting with growth, the birds' lively presence had been replaced by an emptiness far greater than their size, and a silence so loud it was almost a sound in itself. I felt bereft, realizing that one should never take wild birds for granted. I rattled the seed tins, grated cheese, soaked raisins and diced bread. Nothing would induce them to appear. Apparently some people's cats sulk when their owners return from having been away. Mine never sulked. Were the birds sulking? It is not an emotion one associates with birds.

Eventually they relented and gradually started to return. Where had they been, what had they seen and what had they been doing? This time, though, they were accompanied by another form of wildlife, the makers of the molehills: 'field' or 'wood' mice, I called them, because I couldn't bear to think that they might be house mice.

As gardeners they were as bad as Black. The molehills were in fact entrances to a metro system they were busy installing inside the containers. I tried flooding them with a hose but they immediately brought in a metro maintenance team and dug new tunnels. Fortunately their burrowing activities were nocturnal, so although I knew they were there I never saw them, until . . . One warm summer evening I saw a 'field' mouse doing a tight-rope walk across the broom handle en route to the Bird Café. The following evening a mouse slid down the metal feeder guard as though it was practising in a gym.

Before becoming totally panic stricken by the arrival of the mice, to which I am hyper-allergic, I tried to find out what sort they were, naively believing that field and wood mice were preferable because they have large ears, emotional eyes, are vegetarian and prefer to live outdoors. I rang the Natural History Museum, hoping that they would say they were anything but house mice. They suggested I should look them up on the Web

and compare the pictures. I didn't like to admit that I can't even bear looking at mouse pictures, let alone dwelling on their differences. The museum quickly put an end to my field/wood mice preference by saying that they are not fussy where they live as long as it is warm. Equally disturbing was to be informed that their tails are probably even longer than those of house mice. If mice didn't have these long, generally semi-naked, trailing tails they wouldn't be so bad. Also, if they could only amble or saunter along instead of dashing everywhere, it would be a great improvement.

I then rang the RSPB. Was I the only person running a café for birds and mice? Were the two inseparable? Surely I wouldn't have to do anything as drastic as closing the café. What did other people do?

They advised cutting down on the catering, i.e. reducing it to a one-course meal once a day, preferably an early breakfast with only one sitting. What was essential was to clear up thoroughly after breakfast, leaving nothing for the mice. I followed the RSPB's suggestions.

I then had to go away for a fortnight, which I knew would involve the initial bird sulking period on my return, but at least the roof garden should be mouse free.

Fourteen days later I returned late at night after a long flight. Fortunately I pulled back the duvet cover, rather than just plunging into bed. Curled up comfortably in the middle of the bed was a very surprised, half-asleep mouse, which had obviously been using the bed as an en-suite bedroom. But this wasn't the only place the mice had visited.

I tried various methods to encourage them to leave. But they, like the blue tits, were now using the cat flap and no longer darting about, but just strolling around. Unfortunately, the only solution was the council's pest control department. They brought little cup-cake-size saucers of bright turquoise poison, which they distributed round the flat. The mice ate the poison as though it was a dessert.

A couple of weeks later the problem resolved itself: I was adopted by yet another cat-flap visitor. I was busy cooking and looked down to see a stray cat looking intently up at me, as though at a cookery demonstration. Since then we have been happily mice-less but sadly bird-less.

Seeds to sow now, indoors

Apart from all-year-round parsley, and possibly tomatoes, there are a few other seeds that can be sown this month, though don't be tempted to do this too early. Seedlings don't like the cold, or standing around on a windowsill becoming leggy before being taken outside. Those who live on the Shetland Islands will start sowing later than those on the Scilly Isles.

Garlic chives (February–April)
Basil, bush (*Ocimum minimum*) (February–April)
Basil, sweet (*Ocimum basilicum*) (February–April)
Alpine strawberry (*Fragaria vesca* 'Semperflorens') (February)
Busy Lizzies (*Impatiens walleriana*) (mid-February–April)

WHAT TO EAT NOW

Ten-minutes-to-prepare Roman bread

This recipe is a good way to exercise hands in preparation for all the work they will be doing during the following months in the allotment. It is called Ten-minute Roman bread because this is the time it takes to weigh out the ingredients, mix and knead them. The rest of the work (apart from the rising which the dough does on its own) is done by the oven.

1 lb (450 g) organic Spelt flour
(*Triticum spelta*, an ancient precursor of modern wheat varieties)

1 x ¼ oz (7g) sachet Easy-Bake or Fast-Action yeast

1 tsp (5 ml) sea salt

1 tbsp (15 ml) sunflower or olive oil

¾ pint (425ml) warm water – ¼ pint or 150 ml of boiling water from the kettle, the rest from the cold tap; this mixture gives just the right temperature

Preheat the oven to 190°C/375°F/Gas mark 5. Oil a baking tray measuring approximately 13 x 9in (33 x 23cm). Place the flour, yeast, salt and oil in a large bowl. Mix gently. Add the water bit by bit while stirring with your hand. Some flours are 'thirstier' than others. When the dough ball leaves the sides of the bowl, turn on to a flat surface and knead until the dough feels springy. Form into a ball – or any other shape you like. Place in the centre of the tray. Cover with a clean cloth and leave to rise in a warm place (i.e. near the oven). The rising will take 30–45 minutes. Bake in the preheated oven on a middle shelf for 30–35 minutes. A cooked loaf will sound hollow when tapped underneath. Cool the loaf on a wire rack. Resist slicing the bread until it is completely cold.

Variations

You can try different flours, using half white and half brown, all white or all brown flour, adding rye flour, cornmeal or other grains. A whole variety of seeds, nuts and fruits can be included when mixing the dough. These include: poppy seeds (black and white), pumpkin seeds (with or without a tamari coating), sesame seeds, sunflower seeds, sunflower hearts, hazelnuts, pine nuts, almonds, walnuts, brazils, raisins, currants, sultanas and olives (black and green). Nuts and seeds can be toasted or untoasted. A generous handful or two will be sufficient. The surface of the loaf can be left bare or, just before it is put into the oven, sprinkled with flour or painted with egg yolk or white. The surface can also be quickly and gently wetted with warm water – just sufficient to make seeds or grains stick. It can then be sprinkled with sesame seeds, poppy seeds, polenta, soaked wheat grains, cracked wheat or golden linseed.

March

The insect I would least like to be: a captive mealworm

The favourite bird food of some bird-feeder owners (and some fishermen, too) are live mealworms contained in plastic tubs. In this captive state mealworms live, if it can be called 'living', the most miserable of lives.

If being used as bird food, they first travel by post from supplier to customer, being bumped around in an airless container, going they know not where. On arrival they are put into a refrigerator to shiver their days away. If they are lucky, and this is probably rare, they may be given a bran snack; otherwise they will be put on a starvation diet. They will then be brought out and placed on a bird feeder which has straight sides to prevent escape, so should really be called a prison. Here, if they are fortunate, they will soon be eaten alive by a bird or an errant mouse. Alternatively, they will slowly be scorched to death in the sun or drowned in rainwater. Sometimes they can be found lying next to their blackened, dead companions.

It was when a friend gave me a handful of mealworms that I observed these unpleasant facts. I watched an escapee mealworm which had fallen from the bird feeder to the ground – the human equivalent of falling from the Eiffel Tower. Fortunately the mealworm had no bones to break and was wisely hastening away as fast as possible. Considering it only has six front legs (as far as I can see) and glides along like a horizontal escalator, its speed and determination are admirable. It was then that I became interested in mealworms.

When not being superintended by so-called *human* beings, mealworms live most interesting and varied lives – more varied than ours. Unlike us, they undergo four distinct stages in their lives en route to becoming darkling or flour beetles: *Tenebrio molitor*.

Stage One, eggs Mealworms begin life as oval-shaped eggs which are 'glued' on to leaves so that they stand upright. Between a week and a month after being laid, the eggs hatch, when they change not only their shape but their name, too, becoming larvae or grubs, i.e. mealworms.

Stage Two, larvae or grubs During this time, the larva looks nothing like the adult. It has a long body, while the adult's body is rounded in shape. Between bouts of eating vegetation and dead insects, mealworm larvae undergo repeated moults, as they become too big for their exoskeletons and have to change into larger-sized skins.

They can have as many as fourteen moults. Sometimes you can see their discarded skins, which look rather like diaphanous, striped nightgowns. During its last moult, the larva loses its carapace before curling into its pupal (cocoon) form. Larvae have no compound eyes, antennae or wings but they do have a few front feet which help them to wiggle through the soil.

During this stage, when the mealworms are in captivity, their greedy so-called 'caretakers' feed them with hormones to increase their size.

Stage Three, pupa, the resting stage This is the most extraordinary period in a mealworm's life. Gradually the pupa develops a hard outer shell – a carapace. During this time it barely moves or eats. In fact it appears to be dead. But inside its dead-looking exterior, a miraculous metamorphosis is taking place. Its body is breaking down into a kind of soup, being totally dissolved before it is rebuilt and reshaped into an adult winged beetle.

P.S. The other day I was pricking out some chervil seedlings and encountered a most intriguing beetle ambling through the chervil undergrowth. Blackish in colour with lighter flecks, its ribbed shell made it resemble a creature from the prehistoric department of a natural history museum, or a Japanese warrior with a shield. I rushed to get my magnifying glass, but of course the warrior had moved on. Don't imagir these creatures will wait for you to observe them; they have plenty of other things to do. *Always* carry a magnifying glass.

Fourth parsley check

As soon as the parsley seedlings have developed their first two true leaves, it is time to prick them out into more spacious individual accommodation. This can be obtained in various forms: recycled plastic modules (i.e. child-sized yoghurt pots), biodegradable plant trays or containers made from old newspapers using a pot maker (see page 170, A). This is a minute wooden press (which would also be suitable for making fezzes for Egyptian dolls). No glue or skill is required and the newspaper eventually blends into the soil after the seedling has been transplanted.

If using pre-punched plastic modules, make certain that the drainage h has been properly punched; otherwise the module will become waterlogge and would you like to live in a bog? Half-fill the individual containers with compost, making a small hollow to receive the seedling. With a teaspoon, gently scoop out a plant from the original container, taking care not to hurt the roots; they have been just as busy underground as the stem and leaf hav been above.

Don't hold the plant by its stem – this is the most delicate part; holding here is the equivalent of hoisting someone up by the neck. If the seedling m be touched, hold the leaves carefully and, with forefinger and thumb (whic suddenly feel gigantic and Gulliverish), gently place the Lilliputian seedlin in the centre of its new container. Add more soil until this nearly reaches th top, allowing for it to swell when watered. Gently press down the compost, making certain that the stem is straight and the seedling looks secure and comfortable.

An alternative to the teaspoon method is to break the seed-tray content carefully into single seedling portions, as though breaking a crumbly cake. This probably does less damage to the roots.

'The lilliput, countless armies of the grass'
Walt Whitman (1819–92), 'Carol of Harvest'

This part of gardening must surely bring out the maternal or paternal in the most unmotherly or unfatherly of gardeners.

Pricking out and transplanting are such intimate, gentle and peaceful occupations that they are better performed in silence, the ears unclogged by so-called background music or talk, which fills the foreground and induces a fuzzy semi-listening, semi-seeing state.

As the pricking out of all the other seedlings continues, the window ledge will soon become too small in its new capacity as seedling kindergarten. On either side of my bedroom window frame are two permanent brackets, on to which each spring I put a removable shelf to accommodate all the additional pots. If plastic modules are being used, they can be cut to the width of the shelf. After a time it is difficult to see out of the window, but this doesn't matter for the few weeks during which there is so much to see inside.

Although my flat has central heating, the bedroom radiator is turned off during the propagation season, because it becomes too hot for the seeds and seedlings. This leaves the bedroom on the chilly side, so I now resort to using a small electric fire, placed as far away as possible from the window.

The survivors

Something else to check is last year's late autumnal sowings. After almost disappearing during the most severe months, mitsuba, lamb's lettuce, American land cress, rocket and winter purslane reappear – small and bright green, as though they have been on holiday rather than undergoing the endurance test of winter.

The making of compost

The making of compost (though a less extreme version than that quoted below), as opposed to worm compost, is not only for garden gardeners. To begin, all that is needed is a container with a lid, large enough to store a week's supply of what is inaccurately called 'kitchen waste'.

> 'Martyrs' ashes are the best compost to manure the church.'
>
> Thomas Fuller (1608–61), *The History of the Holy War*

March is a good time to start because it is the month that contains the vernal equinox and heralds the gradual lengthening of the days, making going outside more inviting.

Instead of throwing away potato peel, citrus rind, dead flowers, tea leaves and tea bags – plus all the other detritus that is put into the rubbish bin – use them to replenish and enrich the soil. For those with a well-developed Scrooge-ish side, this particular form of thrift should be especially appealing. Anything that has been alive can be used, though it is advisable not to add the remains of animal and fish corpses or anything cooked as these can attract flies and/or vermin.

Roughly chop up banana skins, etcetera, as though making a very chunky salad for a large animal, and put them into the container. This chopping up might seem a nuisance at first, but isn't really (especially when you think of the landfill-sites-versus-compost debate) and soon becomes a habit.

Composting begins in the container, when the 'salad' starts to ferment, lose its individuality, release its water content, reduce slightly in volume and, mysteriously, become faintly warm as it commences its return to the earth from where it came. It is a sort of ashes-to-ashes process, a metamorphosis in reverse. Some people may find it unappealing, but if you know what is happening and observe it, it becomes interesting.

When the container is full, a large, sturdy, plastic garden-waste sack will be needed with ready-made ventilation holes; alternatively the holes can be made with a paper hole-puncher, or you can buy a ready-made bag called Compost-a-Cube (see page 170, D).

Transfer the contents of the container to the plastic sack. Loosely secure the top and place it outside. Continue the squirrelling-away procedure in the container.

Each time you add more material to the sack, mix everything together. Probably the mixing of compost by hand isn't everyone's cup of tea, but there is nothing really unpleasant about it; in fact, it is most interesting if you remember what the ingredients were, and are now becoming. For those who don't like the idea of touching compost – it is only the idea – wear gloves (see the anti-glove lecture on page 8). Garages supply free plastic gloves that, probably unbeknown to them, are ideal for this purpose. However, it is more interesting to feel the material on your skin. Remind yourself that you are adding to the earth, without which there would be nowhere for us to stand.

'Soil is the breathing skin of the earth.'
Anon.

The inauguration of my first compost heap (before I graduated to the sack) took place in a plastic dustbin, which has a lid that can be secured by two clasps. When the lid was 'locked' and the bin rolled sideways and turned upside down and downside up, it acted like one of the more superior tumbler compost bins. Eventually it became too full, heavy and stuffy, and I moved on to the sack. Nevertheless, it was quite useful for the initial stage.

For those who have friends with lawns, ask for a small bag of mowings. Or get to know a public or private park gardener. Mowed grass creates heat, but if too much is added it clogs up the compost and makes it lumpy. Always sprinkle it on; don't just dump it. Then mix well. What is this mysterious heat? What creates it? Mainly bacteria. As they work away, breaking down the organic material, their energy is released in the form of heat.

Straw is another ingredient that compost likes and which helps aerate it, but as bails of straw are not synonymous with towns, torn-up cardboard may be used instead. Compost does not like shiny *Radio Times* sort of paper.

Add dead plants from the allotment, too, but cut them up. Don't add woody stems or leaves. Leaf composting is quite another branch of compost-making, but only for the patient and young, as it can take several years for leaves to turn into mould. Each weekend open the sack to give it fresh air, and mix it up. After only a few weeks everything will start to sink, become heavier, wetter, darker and unrecognizable, like a very organic hippopotamus-portion of muesli. It is still a long way from being compost, yet an equally long way from banana skins and tea leaves. It is now somewhere in between. Fruit flies may visit it, but they are harmless.

One of the main concerns of amateur compost-makers is: does it smell? This depends on your nose, and although compost could never be mistaken for Chanel No. 5, there is nothing unpleasant about it. What is more unpleasant is today's obsession (when concerned with compost) with everything having to be odour free. How bleak an odour-free world would be!

Preparing containers for sowing

March is the month for the first-time window-box gardener to buy window-boxes and pots. Unless there is room for only one window-box, don't buy anything too big. About 27 x 8 x 8in (70 x 20 x 20cm) is a good size, because even when the box is full of earth and plants, and watered, it is still liftable. Buy organic compost – not the one for seed sowing, but the more adult version for transplanting and planting. You will only have to buy it once if you have a compost sack and wormery. I also add some Arthur Bowers John Innes No. 3 peat-free compost. Put concave crocks (broken flower pots) over the drainage holes in the window-box to allow any water to drain away. Then fill with compost.

If filled window-boxes and pots are already available, remove about 1in (2.5cm) of the tired topsoil (this can be added to the compost sack), empty out the rest and sift through it to remove any old roots and lumps. Add a child's handful of pelletized chicken manure, which resembles dry breakfast cereal, or, better still, use the above with added seaweed – available from some nurseries, garden centres and organic suppliers (see page 170). If you have already made compost and/or worm manure, mix in several large handfuls. This mixture should supply most of the nourishment the plants will need, though later in the year you can apply liquid seaweed, or use it as a foliar feed. Don't be too generous with the fertilizer: this results in horticultural indigestion. Return the refreshed soil to the boxes and pots. Water – but don't flood and create a bog.

My window-boxes are divided into three horizontal 'plots', according to the height and habit of the vegetables: for example, tomatoes in the back row, dwarf French beans in the middle and cut-and-come-again lettuce (or rocket) in the front stalls.

Sowing in a window-box

Take a support cane that is just a bit shorter than the length of the box. Place it on the compost, about 1in (2.5cm) from the edge, and create a furrow to the depth suggested on the seed packet, by pressing the cane down and moving it to and fro sideways, making certain that the soil on either side of the furrow is roughly the same in amount (this will be used for covering the seeds). Place a pinch of seeds in your clean palm and sprinkle sparingly into the furrow. Cover with soil made by the furrowing action. Write the date and the name of the seeds on a label – otherwise you will forget.

Some of the larger seeds, like the wrinkled, worried-looking spinach and the seahorse-tail segments of chard, can be sown individually. Ignore the packet's instructions and sow close together, about 3in (7.5 cm) apart, not 8in (20cm) – there isn't the space to spare and they don't seem to mind living close together. Sow a couple more, just in case any fail to germinate.

With the larger seeds, count how many you have sown and add the amount to the label information. Sometimes you put in six, and up pop eight. With the smaller sprinklable seeds, don't sow too many. You don't want a glut of vegetables. Though the word 'glut' when linked to containers may seem a slight exaggeration, it is not. I've had 'gluts' of tomatoes (despite giving them away to friends and puréeing and freezing them), beans, lettuce and basil. It is better to sow little and often.

Sowing tip: medium-sized seeds (those too small for lifting with finger and thumb) can be sown individually by taking a light-coloured pencil, licking the tip, and then lifting the seed by the dampened tip and transferring it to the compost.

Worm menu

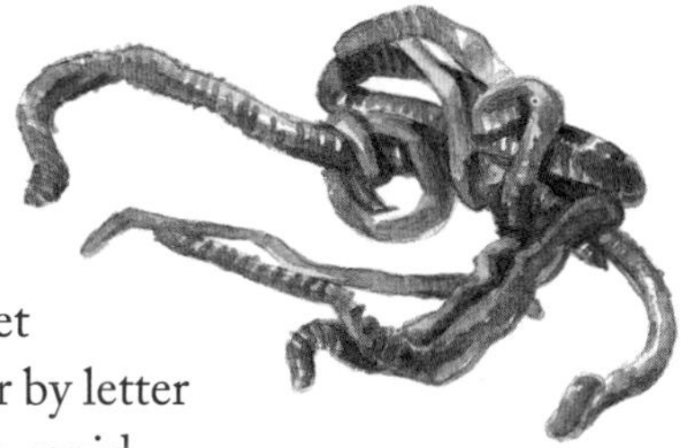

If you have ordered a wormery, the worms' accommodation will arrive first by parcel post, giving time for you to follow the instructions and set it up for the tenants, who will arrive a few days later by letter post. Worms are not generally posted on Fridays, to avoid having them loitering in sorting offices during the weekend.

While waiting for their arrival, start collecting food; they only need a snack at this stage. Compost heaps and wormeries require different diets. This doesn't mean that you have to open a canteen and cater specially for the reds and tigers. They like apple peel, bread, banana skins, baked beans, cabbage stalks and outer leaves, old cake, coffee grounds, outer celery stalks, old cheese, cucumber tops and bottoms, torn-up newspapers, eggshells, egg and milk cartons (soaked first), cold porridge, pasta, pineapple skin, cooked potatoes, plate scrapings, tea leaves and tea bags.

They don't like the peel of lemons, limes or oranges, or onion skins, which are all too acid. They hate nappy liners, grass and cat or dog faeces. As they have no teeth, they prefer to have their food cut up small.

From now on, instead of throwing away eggshells and all the other 'menu' items listed above, start collecting them. The eggshells can be dried in an oven – or let the air do the drying and then crunch them up.

Because they have no teeth, food is ground down in the worms' gizzards. Grains of sand and mineral particles collect in the gizzard, the muscular walls of which contract, compressing the hard particles and food while mixing it with digestive juices and grinding it down. Birds' gizzards work in a similar way, and so do waste-disposal units; did their inventors copy the worms – or birds?

Why do worms need eggshells? Eggshells provide grit and calcium carbonate, which is necessary for reproduction and to prevent the wormery from becoming too acid. Powdered limestone, which does the same job, can be used instead. But eggshells are free, where limestone is not, and when using the latter you miss out on the collecting, drying and grinding process which makes you more a part of the wormery process – an aspect some would perhaps be prepared to sacrifice.

Worms' arrival

When the worms arrive they should be placed in the wormery immediately and allowed to recover from their journey. Don't peep at them: they don't like light and need a little privacy.

Fifth parsley check

As soon as the March air becomes a little warmer and the sun a little stronger, the four-leaved parsley seedlings can be taken for a visit to the outside world – like putting a baby out in its pram for the first time. Before it gets dark, bring in the seedlings. Repeat these 'acclimatization' outings each sunny day.

The first time I (unsuccessfully) grew melons, I took great care to follow my own advice, to the extent that I had to rush home early from a party, suddenly having remembered the stranded melon seedlings freezing to death outdoors.

Arrival of ordered seeds

By now the seeds you ordered should have arrived by letter post. If all the produce they will produce were to be returned – the total harvest of stems, shoots, flowers and fruit – a small van would probably be needed.

The sound of them rattling like small maracas in their slim packets fills you with expectation.

Seeds to sow now, indoors

Aubergine (*Solanum melongena*) 'Slim Jim'
Cape gooseberry (*Physalis peruviana*, syn. *P. edulis*)

Lady in a mosquito net

Cape gooseberry is ideal for tubs as it grows vertically and is perennial; though the seed packet's instructions say 'Grow as a half-hardy annual', there's nothing half-hardy or annual-ish about my physalis. In Arabic it is called Sitt el Namousia, lady in a mosquito net. Each fruit is ensconced in its own private paper lantern. To begin with it is bright green. As it grows larger it becomes paler until much to one's surprise through its paperiness a small yellow 'bulb'-like fruit can be seen. As the lampshade becomes still paler, the fruit becomes larger, brighter and more orange, the lady glowing gently through her mosquito net. If the lantern is left on its stem the sweet-sour fruit becomes smaller, eventually returning to its seed stage, while the lantern changes from paper to Victorian lace. There is nowhere one could buy such a delicately veined and ribbed lantern.

Seeds to sow now, outdoors

Lettuce (*Lactuca sativa*), 'Salad Bowl' and 'Red Salad Bowl'
Perpetual spinach (a member of the beetroot species)
New Zealand spinach (*Tetragonia tetragonioides*)
Swiss chard (*Beta vulgaris* Cicla Group) 'Bright Lights' (a member of the beetroot species)
Mignonette
Nasturtium (*Tropaeolum majus*)
Night-scented stock (*Matthiola longipetala* subsp. *bicornis*)
Virginia stock (*Matthiola incana*) with its minute cinnamon-coloured seed

Some of these seeds (for instance New Zealand spinach and Swiss chard) can also be sown in the autumn when sowing possibilities are more limited. Depending on how much space there is, it may be advisable to keep some of the autumnal germinators until then, though chard in its rainbow version, 'Bright Lights' (sometimes called 'Jacob's Coat' or 'Rainbow' chard), is so appealing that it is worth sowing in both spring and autumn.

The stems and leaf veins of chard may be red, yellow, burgundy, cream or white, the colour almost phosphorescent, appearing to be illuminated from within, seeping up from below. The leaves may only be small and some are a little tough in the early part of the year. This is not surprising, since they have had to combat rain, wind, cold, ice and snow. But they provide a steamed salad that most rabbits would envy, even without a trickling of sesame oil and rice vinegar. Alternatively, instead of being turned into a salad, they can be dropped into simmering vegetable stock. As the year progresses and the weather relents, the plants do likewise and relax, producing a new, tender leaf crop.

WHAT TO EAT NOW

Steamed Swiss chard salad

If leaves are big, cut the stems into 1in (2.5cm) lengths and place on a steamer rack. Cover with leaves. Steam until wilted. Chard is so full of taste and juice that it is delicious eaten as it is, undressed. If this does not appeal, add, while still warm, a trickle of olive, sesame or sunflower oil and either lemon or balsamic or rice vinegar. Eat warm or cold.

April

Growing potatoes

Potatoes can be grown in 8in (20cm) pots, potato barrels or thick plastic sacks. It is too late to order special potatoes now (order in October–November for delivery in December–March). This year you could conduct a trial potato-growing experiment, either with those that start sprouting of their own accord in the bottom of the refrigerator, or by buying seed potatoes from a garden centre.

Early morning inspection

This is a most beneficial activity. Before starting work, go on a 'tour' of all the window-boxes, tubs and pots and see what has happened since you last looked. It is not only we who are busy. New developments take place during the day and night: two leaves have suddenly become three. The bent-over stems of chives are straightening, their tips still weighed down by minute seed coats. Nasturtiums' furled-umbrella leaves are opening. In profile, the sweet peas now resemble meerkats. Tomato stems are furrier, their 'haloes' thickening. The cucumber's third leaf has serrated saw-tooth edges.

It is surely better for the eyes to see and be nourished by these sights than by half-digested horror headlines in the newspapers – those can come later. So can another inspection.

Revisiting the wormery

By now the worms will have settled down and be munching, mating, and producing eggs, worm casts (manure) and liquid manure. The best moment to see them is at feeding time, when the lid is lifted and they are caught unawares: tunnelling through bean-pod interiors, massed together in a worm scrum, gambolling, turning somersaults and being generally playful . . . until they sense the light and within seconds have disappeared, gliding down beneath the compost's surface. A worm's whole body can taste and feel both light and sound. What do light and sound taste and feel like? Are they cool or warm, sweet or savoury? Sometimes, after heavy rain, a few of the younger worms may be found wandering around the lid area. If gently lifted, potential escapees can be returned to the clan. It is surprising how lively they can be, wriggling and squirming like the most wilful child – and all without arms or legs.

'So I went into the garden and ate
three worms, two smooth ones and a hairy one;
the hairy one tickled all the way down.'
Hilaire Belloc (1870–1953)

They can also be quite skittish and coy at times, playing hide-and-seek by popping up and down out of the compost. A lot of life goes on beneath a wormery lid.

'A round little worm pricked from the
lazy finger of a maid.'
William Shakespeare (1564–1616), *Romeo and Juliet*

Idle worms: it was once supposed that little worms were bred in the fingers of idle servants.

Reproduction

As worms are hermaphrodites they have both ovaries and testes, and during reproduction produce both eggs and sperm to fertilize the eggs. When mating, they lie side by side, facing in opposite directions, joined by a mucus-like substance that is produced by the clitellum.

(This is the swollen band, sometimes called the 'saddle' or 'girdle', like a plump pink wedding ring, situated on the thirteenth segment about one-third of the distance between head and tail. It is quite easy to see and indicates that the worm is sexually mature.) Sperm passes from worm to worm. Later, a cocoon forms in the clitellum of each worm. Before the cocoons harden, the worms wriggle out backwards. As they do so, sperm and eggs are deposited in the cocoons as they pass over the openings of the ovaries and sperm storage sacs. When the cocoons are released from the worms (they drop off the ends, where the worms' 'noses' should be) they close up at both ends and egg fertilization takes place inside. A worm cocoon is about the size of a grain of wheat, lemon shaped, a translucent yellow-green in colour and could be mistaken for a tomato pip.

After a couple of weeks one or two baby worms will hatch from one end of the cocoon. After a year the babies will be fully grown.

When touched, some young slim worms behave in a most un-wormlike way. Suddenly these burrowers and gliders become like watch springs released from their cases, twisting, turning, coiling and uncoiling, sometimes millimetres above the ground.

Planting beans

This is the time for sowing one of the most dramatic of germinators: beans. Dwarf French beans can be sown outside in May and runners from May to June, but they can also be sown inside now, where they can be observed more closely. Either plant runner beans in saved-up toilet-roll interiors or in deepish (3in or 7.5cm at least) saved-up plastic containers. Make a hole with your finger, about 1½in (4cm) deep (see the packet instructions), and place the bean inside, with its scar facing downwards. This is the point from which the root emerges. If placed the right way up (or, rather, down) to begin with, it saves the bean from having to swivel round.

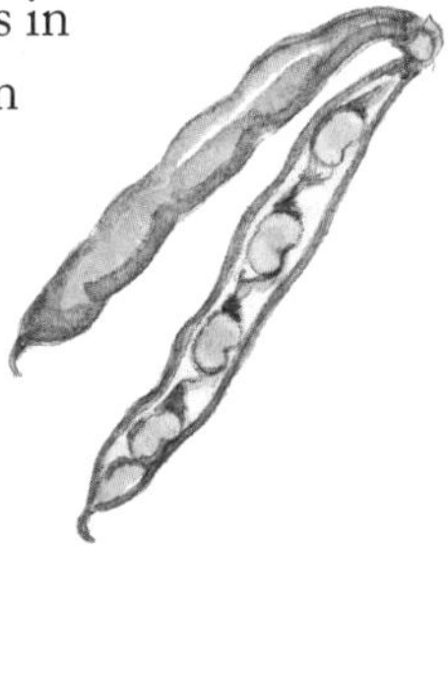

Hanging baskets

As well as window-boxes, pots and tubs, hanging baskets make good receptacles for vegetables. Don't line them with that hideous, faded-green padded plastic or the equally unattractive and quickly disintegrating carpet underlay or old doormat fibre, but with moss, which can be bought in packets. One of its main advantages is the pleasure to be had from laying it out in the basket: it is the closest most of us will come to knowing what it is like to make a nest. Admittedly, after a short time and despite watering, its mossy greenness disappears and it becomes straggly and lacy. Hanging baskets are filled with the same compost that is used for window-boxes and pots. Any of the smaller vegetables will grow quite comfortably in them. Mine have been inhabited by alpine strawberries and a 'herb grove': three rows of bush basil (bushy with tiny leaves) at one end, three rows of sweet basil (larger leaves) at the other, separated by two rows of dill. Earlier in the year huge bouquets of frizzy endive dwarfed the baskets.

A favourite aversion

Something that I particularly enjoy disliking at the moment is the proliferation of those fashionable, sarcophagi-shaped containers. Usually they are made of very matt metal, highly glazed ceramic or icy-to-the-touch aluminium and are battleship grey, navy blue, black or some other cheerful colour. Although they probably have sufficient soil to support a mini apple tree, normally all they contain is a painfully pruned (from a distance resembling a tight perm or crew cut) gloomy green, spherical blob of box.

Why do people like, or why are they persuaded that they like, these strict, straight-sided, proportionally absurd containers? The box plants live or, rather, survive in solitary confinement in these vertical mini coffins. They are advertised as low-maintenance plants, i.e. needing minimum care and little water – the latter probably because there is not much difference in appearance between when they are dead or alive. In other words, why bother to have a plant at all? When will low-maintenance pets, partners and children be available?

Potato watch

Potatoes should be happily chitting away in their eggbox, their shoots growing longer and sturdier. No matter when Easter is, I like to plant them on Good Friday, when the Devil is supposed to be busy elsewhere.

Sunshine outings

As soon as the sun comes out, load all the different seed containers and seedlings on to trays and take them outside. When it becomes cooler and darker, return them to the window-ledge shelf.

Sixth parsley check

By now the seedlings should be ready to transplant into one of the pots, tubs or window-boxes. Unless you have become a serious eater of parsley, or a specialist, there is no need to plant them in window-box rows – just here and there between other plants.

Don't bother with a trowel when transplanting seedlings into containers. The soil is friable and hands are more malleable than tools – and it is more enjoyable to touch the plants. Burrow a comfortable-looking hole into the soil, about the size of the parsley container, then put in the seedling, firming the soil until it looks secure and the stem is straight. Water and leave.

Next morning check to see that the seedling hasn't been blown over, or is keeling over because of thirst or not having been planted deep enough.

The first night out

By now the other seedlings will have done a lot of to-ing and fro-ing on their stretcher-trays between indoors and out. As soon as a warmish evening feels imminent, they can spend their first night out to complete the acclimatization. At this stage in their life they should be able to stand up to a gentle watering from above from a watering can with a fine rose.

Runner bean watch

This is hardly necessary, as beans make such a soundless commotion when germinating that even the most unobservant seed sower couldn't fail to notice that something is happening.

The first time I grew beans I couldn't understand why each morning a little compost was scattered on the window ledge beside the container. Had wind blown it there? Or were the cats testing the compost as an alternative to litter? Day by day the compost disturbance increased. What was taking place was more of an upheaval than germination, as the beans pushed upwards, hardly able to wait to emerge from the compost. (Some seeds are even capable of pushing up asphalt and concrete.)

Final parsley check: reaping what has been sown

Apart from thinning the seedlings during pricking out, no real tasting has yet taken place. Since then the stems have thickened, lengthened and filled with more sap, while the leaves have broadened and multiplied. To reap what one has sown is a triumphant moment. And the more you pick, the more the parsley will grow.

No matter how much parsley is sown, there is never enough. Sow more.

Strawberry propagation

Strawberry runners (those long trailing stems coming from the main plant and tipped with a small clump of bright leaves) are not so easy to propagate when grown in tubs or window-boxes, as there is not enough space. But if you create a halfway house, a type of kindergarten container, propagation is possible.

When the runners start running, fill a container approximately 12in (30cm) in diameter and 5in (13cm) deep with compost, and support it on an upturned bucket or something similar about 12–20in (30–50cm) below the container where the parent plant lives. Now wait for the runners to lower themselves down to the new container. When they have reached just a couple of centimetres below their destination, make a small indentation in the compost. Gently press in the base of the leaf tufts but don't smother them. This is where the new roots will come from. With a hairpin or homemade hairpin-shaped piece of bent wire, secure them in the compost about ¾in (2cm) away from the leaves. Do *not*, yet, sever either the main umbilical cord attaching the young strawberry to the parent plant or the secondary potential propagating runner. After a short time, new leaves will emerge from the secured offspring. Now the umbilical cord can be cut a couple of centimetres above the new leaves. A new strawberry plant begins its life. Endless plants can be propagated from the runners and the runners' runners.

Seeds to sow now, indoors

Dwarf French bean (*Phaseolus vulgaris*) – 'Sprite' is good
Runner bean (*Phaseolus coccineus*) 'Scarlet Emperor'
Cucumber (*Cucumis sativus*) 'Simpson's Sweet Success'
Dill (*Anethum graveolens*)

Seeds to sow now, outdoors

American land cress (*Barbarea verna*) – or save for August sowing
Komatsuna – or save for September sowing
Lettuce (*Lactuca sativa*) 'Black Seeded Simpson'
Rocket (*Eruca versicaria* subsp. *sativa*)
Oriental saladini
Vegetable amaranth (dark-grey caviar-like seeds)
Iceland poppy

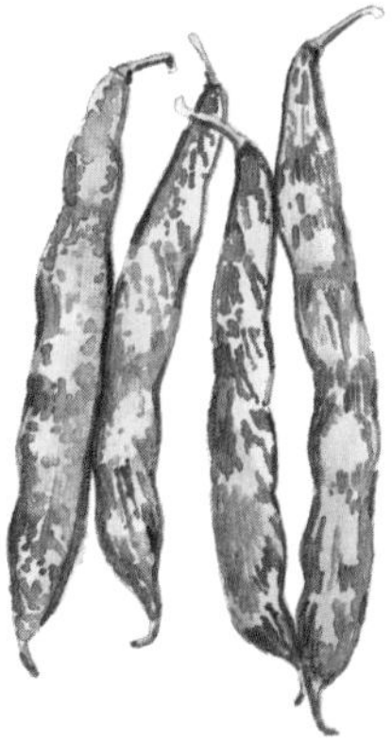

WHAT TO EAT NOW

Cold chicken consommé with sour cream and black lumpfish 'caviar'

1 x 400ml tin of the best chicken consommé you can find, preferably organic

1 small carton (approx. 200ml) of sour cream or crème fraîche

1 small jar (approx. 200ml) of black lumpfish caviar

small handful of dill or tarragon

Put the tin of consommé into the refrigerator until almost solid. Then divide between two soup bowls. Top with a generous helping of sour cream, lumpfish and finely chopped herbs. Eat the consommé while still in its jelly-ish state. Don't wait until it has liquefied.

May

Making a pond

Plants are so generous in nourishing our senses – sight, taste, touch and smell – that I hadn't realized, until sitting beside a friend's spacious rooftop pond and its fountain, that sound was the only sense missing from my roof garden. It has the reassuring buzz of bees and the deliciously watery sounds made by birds deciding which of the 'orchard' plums to eat; what is missing is the cool trickling and light splashing of water – especially refreshing when heard in the centre of a city.

I had always looked down on artificial ponds, associating them with eternally fishing gnomes and hollow, fibreglass rocks. I had also wrongly assumed that having a pond involved filters, bungs and other underwater equipment. My rooftop friend assured me that this was not so and that a mini-pump fountain is simple to install. It was – in about half an hour.

Before skipping this part of the book, thinking that your balcony is too small, wait. Even the smallest balcony – just deep enough for two feet to stand on – can have a fountain and/or a pond. Windowsill owners can have small fountains or waterfalls. And for those living in flat-chested flats without window ledges who are desperate for the sound of water, there are indoor tabletop fountains.

Wall-mounted, puffed-cheeked, dribbling cherubs, lions and goddesses or incontinent boys do not make particularly attractive waterfalls, though at least the boys make more sense than the others. The simplest and easiest method is to put the pump inside an imitation-terracotta plastic tub. It has to be plastic, a) because of the weight and b) because containers without ready-made drainage holes are hard to find. These drainage holes are marked on the plastic and left for the owner to drill or not drill.

My tub is hexagonal in shape, 16in (40cm) in diameter and 9in (23 cm) deep, so there's no danger of drowning. Being plastic, a hole was easily drilled in it, about 1in (2.5cm) from the top, to allow the pump flex to pass through.

So far all that is needed is a 'mini-cascade' pump, a plastic tub (yours could be smaller than mine) and an RCD (residual current device) to protect against electric shocks – all available from most garden centres.

The fountain has three settings. The lowest and narrowest is 'Intimate Evening', the tallest and widest 'Blackpool Lights' and the third 'Upturned Jelly'. With an additional piece of plastic hose there could also be a waterfall.

The surface of my tub-pond was going to be covered with chicken wire to support big pebbles and stones, creating a pseudo-Japanese effect. Then, while looking at the bare face of the water, I wondered about aquatic plants – an aspect of gardening that had always seemed totally alien to earth gardening, and unachievable on a rooftop. However, a few hours later, after reading about ponds, I was walking round an aquatic garden centre – something else that I didn't know existed.

Now, floating on and growing over the edges of the tub are a pygmy waterlily, which promises to produce pink flowers (it comes with a guarantee); creeping Jenny, which has yellow buttercup-like flowers; cotton grass – untidy wispy heads, which look bedraggled after rain and badly blow-dried when dry; floating beaver with, appropriately, beaver-shaped, almost furry-looking, boat-like leaves; and parrot's feather, with its fluffy-duster-ish leaf. The above list makes it sound more like a zoo than a pond. If it were larger, frogbit, water crowfoot, turtlehead, scarlet monkey flower, toad lily, skunk cabbage and zebra rush could also be added. Apart from the above list, also available are sweet flag, brandy bottle, Joe Pye weed, submerged water soldier, fairy moss, yellow floating heart or water fringe, arrowhead, bugle, and many more whose names are as intriguing as the plants.

Alternatively, there are plastic waterlilies, guaranteed 'to beautify your pond all year round' and no doubt machine washable.

Aquatic plants are divided into five types: 'free-floaters', 'marginals', 'oxygenators', 'fixed-floating aquatics' and 'waterlilies'. Sounding far more knowledgeable than I am, I can now discuss with other pond owners the merits of free-floaters and marginals versus oxygenators and fixed-floaters, enjoying these five new additions to my vocabulary. I had not imagined that something that is only 16 x 16 x 9in (40 x 40 x 23cm) filled with water, plants and a fountain could also contain so much pleasure. I visit it several times a day to see what is going on. A lot is (see the June chapter).

The last of the five senses, hearing, is satisfied.

Good Friday potatoes

The Good Friday potatoes should now be breaking through the surface of the compost, their tips green. As they ascend, add more soil, covering stems but not tips.

The orchard

The orchard will now be in full sail with blossom. It is quite difficult for an uninitiated eye to tell the difference between pear, plum and cherry blossom. Now is the time to find out. Insects are visiting the blossom; the lonely self-fertilizer is making the best of a bad job, preparing to perform the equivalent of an immaculate conception.

Tomato plant roots

If tomato plants were sown in the transparent supermarket trays, by now they will have been transplanted into individual pots. It is then, and while in the transparent trays, that their roots can be observed, growing many times as long as their stems, but only a fraction as thick. This underground root world we know so little about is just as interesting. Over, round and through compost obstacles – lumps and bumps – they go in search of minerals, salts and water, fragile but determined.

Making more space

Remove the older-generation vegetables. Some, such as frizzy endive, become bitter after a time and although they may still look splendid, it is time to remove them. The hanging basket they occupy will be needed for alpine strawberries.

Vegetable bouquets

When removing senior vegetables, don't just put them straight on to the compost heap. Let them spend time in a wide-mouthed bowl as a bouquet. The frizzy endives' bright light-green frilly leaves will fill and froth over the bowl.

Compost: to activate or not

To return to the compost heap and the question of whether to add an activator (something which hurries up the process of decomposition) or not. Some people do, some don't. Organic activators can be bought, though one of the best doesn't need to be. We all possess it: urine. On discovering this, I immediately knew that I was a latent night-soil type and whether the heap needed it or not it received its activator. Mix one part of urine with four parts (some say seven) of water. It must be diluted as otherwise it is too strong. Use an old plastic spray bottle to disperse the activator.

First salad feast

The 'Salad Bowl' lettuce leaves should be ready. Remove carefully one by one from the stem. Some people cut the hearts out, leaving an inch of leaves below, and wait for new leaves to grow. Rocket should also be ready. Its taste is decisive, even in the smallest leaves.

Usually I don't wash the plants I have grown, preferring to eat them as soon as they are picked, even though they might contain an insect or two. I would rather eat a couple of insects by mistake than eat lambs' tongues or pigs' trotters on purpose.

Planting plan

This may seem a little grandiose for a few pots and boxes and more applicable to the high-yield, no-taste-no-texture Dutch methods of cultivation. But it is not. One soon forgets what is growing where and will probably end up with too many beans or too few aubergines.

Sketch a little plan of the boxes and pots, jotting down what each contains (i.e. ten 'Sprite' beans in the back row, 'Salad Bowl' lettuce in the front, sweet basil at both ends).

Sowing outside is similar to sowing inside but on a larger scale. Whether it is in pots or boxes, the soil must be friable, its surface even. Some seeds, like night-scented stock, need to be raked into the surface. This can be done with a long-haired cat's wide-toothed grooming comb which resembles a miniature rake. When sowing individual seeds, like beans, which need depth, take a pencil or cane, mark the end with the required depth and make the hole. Some seeds need to be sown in drills (a shallow furrow). Lay a pencil or cane on the surface, push it to and fro to indicate the drill. If the drill needs to be deeper, make your four fingertips walk sideways along the drill while pressing downwards and deepening it, creating little mounds on either side to cover the seeds when sown. Always sow a few more than necessary in case some fail to germinate.

Runner bean watch

The once neatly patted-down surface of the soil continues to swell and rise, creating fissures and ravines. As the beans force their way upwards, pitted boulders roll away, landing on the window ledge. The beans' sturdy stem necks are still lowered, their solid 'heads' gradually emerging like young heifers'. This is more like a Stanley Spencer resurrection than just eight beans germinating in an ex-Waitrose peach container. It is advisable to arrange one's day around this event rather than relying on the occasional visit.

May – the loveliest of months

It is always sad when the maternity-ward window-ledge shelf is taken down in May and put away for next year: another spring has gone. There is a lot to be done at this time of year and although the days are longer now, they never seem long enough and by midday half the day has already gone and one longs to elongate what remains.

If it rains, don't stop gardening, just put up a garden umbrella: the drops are usually warm, gentle and spaced wide apart.

Second sowings

This is the month to make second sowings. It is tricky to know when to do this to avoid having too much of one vegetable. One method is to sow the second crop as soon as the first has reached the eating stage and you are sure you like it. Some gardeners make repeat sowings every fortnight. I started doing this, jotting the dates down in my diary – 'Sow more 'Salad Bowl' lettuce now', etc. – until the diary began to look as though it belonged to a rabbit.

When going to a garden centre to buy seeds rather than ordering them by post (owing to insufficient patience), it is sad to see people wheeling away trolley-loads of already-in-bloom plants, the trolleys three-quarters empty of the enjoyment of sowing.

The Cretans

In May, several years ago, I was in Crete, crossing a main road. The road was divided in two by knee-high, sturdy-leaved bushes bearing ivory-coloured, waxy-petalled flowers whose yellow centres looked as though they had sucked in the strong Greek sun. But it was their delectable scent which was most seductive. Reminiscent of gardenia, it could almost have been eaten with a spoon.

Beneath the bushes were some of the plants' seeds. While the cars sped past on the left and right, I gathered seeds. They were the size of milk teeth and felt more like pebbles, something from the mineral rather than the plant kingdom.

The following spring I sowed them, in London, in a propagator on a bedroom windowsill. Nothing happened. Two weeks later I examined one of the seeds and saw that probably only a pre-soaking would make its rock-hard coat relent and open. I put them in tepid water, hoping they would mistake it for a warm Greek shower. They didn't. Their Minoan stubbornness persisted. Only after a week's soaking did they begin to open. I sowed them for a second time.

Once they had germinated, despite their alien surroundings they started to flourish. When they were past the seedling stage, they were moved to a larger pot. As the weather became warmer, they were taken on to my roof garden for sunbathing outings, returning them to the windowsill at dusk. After a few more weeks they progressed to single pots and were allowed to stay out all night.

Taller and larger they grew, cheerfully producing leaf after unwanted (by me) leaf, making up for their reluctant germination. As my roof garden measures 8 x 16ft (2.5 x 5m), I began to wonder what I was going to do with this potential forest. So, rather grandiosely, I started to offer them to carefully selected friends, providing them with details of the plants' lineage, colour and scent plus germination details. Despite the seductive descriptions of their scent, I noticed that no one leapt at the opportunity of adopting one of the somewhat dull-looking plant refugees. But I persisted and in the end several found homes in real gardens.

Then followed another long waiting period. To be honest, about five flowerless years passed. The bushes were suffering from amnesia and had obviously forgotten how to bloom, so to compensate, concentrated entirely on producing greenery, which was all very well but not what I had expected. I didn't want to look a gift horse in the mouth, but where was that scent, the flowers and their yellow centres?

As each spring came and passed, I almost gave up looking to see if there were any buds. Then, this year, to my astonishment and delight, there they were, tightly folded, secretive and ready to bloom in the same month as they bloom on Crete. I couldn't wait to ring the Cretans' adopters.

At the same moment, one of them happened to ring me and ask in a somewhat impatient tone, 'What exactly is that rather dull Greek plant supposed to *do*?' I didn't need to be clairvoyant to know that the Cretan was within inches of being lopped, so I begged for a stay of execution.

After a few days, the phone rang again and a delighted voice announced that the plant was in bud.

Although the London version of the flowers' centres is more akin to single than double cream, in texture they are just as beautiful and waxy and the scent just as delicious as it wafts down the passage stairs from the roof garden, accompanied by the scent of jasmine and honeysuckle. A Greek friend told me it is *angeliki* (*Pittosporum tobira*).

Seeds to sow now, outdoors

Abyssinian mustard, also know as Texsel greens (or leave until later for an autumn sowing)
Beetroot (*Beta vulgaris*) 'Detroit 2-Tardel'
Lettuce (*Lactuca sativa*) 'Catalogna'
Mizuna, also known as Japanese greens (again, this could be sown in the autumn)
Mitsuba, also known as Japanese parsley (can also be sown in August)

WHAT TO EAT NOW

Chinese sweet-sour radish salad

20 small radishes
½ tsp (2.5ml) sea salt
1 tsp (5ml) soy sauce
2 tsp (10ml) rice vinegar
1 tbsp (15ml) sesame oil
1 tbsp (15ml) sesame seeds, toasted

Top and tail the radishes. If young and tender, cut the green tops into half-inch lengths. Using a heavy implement smash the radishes, but not into smithereens; you should still be able to pick them up in one piece. Mix together all the ingredients except the sesame seeds to make the dressing. Marinate the radishes in the dressing for a couple of hours. Sprinkle with the toasted sesame seeds.

June

Growing saffron

Between June and August the saffron (*Crocus sativus*) corms (underground swollen stem bases) bought in February can be planted. They like to live in sunny, sheltered places; they dislike shade. You will need 9–10in (23–25cm) deep pots. Fill them with organic multi-purpose compost plus a handful or two of homemade compost, worm casts and a sprinkling of pelletized chicken manure. For those who have pH soil testers (used to measure the soil's acidity) the pH level should be about seven. The addition of a little lime may help the soil to reach this level, or use ground eggshells (see page 44).

The corms are planted 6in (15cm) deep and 4in (10cm) apart to give them space for reproduction. All the above measurements are just right for containers. Between planting time and September the corms won't object to being on the dry side (remember the other places where they flourish, such as Kashmir and Spain). In September, they will need watering to help the roots grow. In October the first shoots will appear – the right month to have something to look forward to when most other plants are dying down. The soil has to reach a temperature of 41°F (5°C) in order to shock the corms into flowering. This is similar to oyster mushrooms, which also need the shock of coldness to persuade them to fruit – hence their sojourn in the refrigerator (see page 155). What is this need for iciness before fruition?

Flowering should continue for about three weeks. The suppliers of the corms say that it is better to pick the flowers when they are closed, as the saffron will be more intense. In Spain they are picked when open. The drying of the stigma, quite a simple process, is described in a booklet that accompanies the corms – or the La Mancha method could be tried (see page 110).

After flowering ceases, the leaves continue to flourish. From November until April corm reproduction takes place. In May, after all the activity of flowering, producing leaves and reproducing the corms, the leaves die. The plants then need a rest and a retreat. The corms become dormant, their development suspended. Is this similar to the hibernation of animals, when animation is suspended, and to our sleep, which suspends most activity? But when sleep is interspersed with dreams it can hardly be called dormant. Are these three periods related? If so, perhaps more is going on at this time in plants, animals and us than we know.

It is during the dormant period that, every four years, the corms should be lifted, the old ones removed and the new ones sorted, cleaned and dried, ready for replanting.

The first year's flowers are apt to be a bit sparse, but in the second and third year, as the corms increase in number, so should the flowers.

1. February: order saffron corms.
2. June–August: plant corms.
3. September: water containers to encourage the roots to grow. Look up saffron recipes.
4. October: flowers and leaves appear. Harvesting and drying. First taste. Harvesting may continue into November.
5. November–April: leaves still green, corms reproducing.
6. May: leaves dying down. Corms become dormant, sleeping. Do not disturb.
7. May, four years later: lift corms, clean, sort and dry.
8. June: the story begins again.

Horticultural shepherding

At this time of year everything is gaining momentum, making one realize how short summer is and how important it is to observe it and take note. This is the month that contains one of the loveliest, yet one of the saddest, days, 21 June, the summer solstice and the longest day, whose next-door neighbour, 22 June, begins the descent towards the winter solstice and the shortest, darkest day. However, to cheer oneself up, don't forget that the next-door neighbour of the winter solstice begins the ascent towards spring.

As you are a kind of horticultural shepherd, each day needs to be checked for what is happening and to make certain that all is well. For example, in one 27 x 8 x 8in (70 x 20 x 20cm) window-box grows a row of rocket, a row of 'Sprite' beans, a row of perpetual spinach and a row of 'Catalogna' lettuce, which equals thirty-six plants all needing different attention. Tomatoes now require supporting with canes; their in-between shoots (the shoot between the main stem and side shoot) need to be removed to stop them from pushing all their energy into becoming bushes. At the same time cover the tips of all the support canes with silver foil to prevent damaging your eyes (tall *Lilium regale* stems make good supports). When securing stems to support canes, use old-fashioned twine: it is softer and gentler on stems than plastic or metal.

Some small plants may be a bit leggy. Whether the following suggestion is horticulturally correct or incorrect, I don't know. But it works. With a dibber (a hand tool with a pointed end for making holes) *gently* remove a leggy plant from the soil and replant it a little deeper to make it more comfortable. I emphasize 'gently' because quite a few television gardeners handle plants rather roughly, just plonking them into a hole and shovelling the soil around as though there's no time to spare. Kittens or Spode china wouldn't be treated in this way. The dibber is one of the most useful of window-box gardening tools. Mine is a variation on the theme, between a generous Stilton spoon and a shoehorn for narrow feet. By placing it into the soil and moving it backwards and forwards, you create a pocket into which you can slip a small plant. If dwarf French beans and 'Salad Bowl' lettuce have been sown in the same box, the big butterfly-shaped leaves of the beans and the bosky lettuce may be creating too much shade: trim a few of the lower bean leaves and nibble-prune the largest lettuce leaves to make more light.

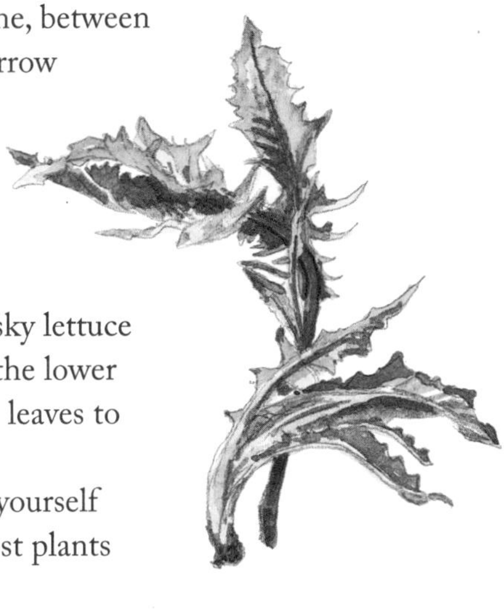

Always try to water plants before 'watering' yourself with a breakfast coffee or an evening drink. Most plants can't turn on taps.

Confession number two: the pond

Having a pond opens your eyes to other ponds, one of which (situated in a well-known garden) I was passing after having installed mine. And 'passing' is what I should have continued doing. Covering this pond's surface was a thick bright green plant, so dense that at first it appeared to be solid: a flat surface covered with bouclé-knitted lichen. I endeavoured to convince myself that the pond was suffering from overcrowding and that a very little light pruning of this plant (equal to about a tablespoon) wouldn't do any harm and might do some good. Aware that what I was doing was more akin to stealing than pruning, I was relieved that I didn't fall into the pond while committing this act. It was so tempting that I was about to step on to it. Fortunately my forefinger discovered that beneath the 'knitting' was a pond. I slipped the 'pruning' into my handbag, wondering how it would survive the waterless journey home and the handbag environment.

As soon as I got back, I immediately placed the 'pruning' (called 'Stolen Goods') in the tub-pond, where it made a remarkable recovery . . . a bit too remarkable, because now, only a few weeks later, the thimbleful is mounting the sides of the pond and threatening to submerge the lily pads.

Making logs

This Royal Borough's (free) *Kensington and Chelsea Times* not only converts into plant pots, can be added to compost and also used as a wormery 'blanket'. Then there is another useful job for it, and this is to be recycled into logs for burning on a fire. It is just the right size, 15 x 12in (40 x 30cm). Any unglossy newspaper may be used – it doesn't have to be royal. As soon as the weather becomes warmer (the 'logs' need to dry in the sun) the log-making can begin.

First you need to buy a Log Maker (see page 170, I) which will mould the newspaper into a log shape. Most of the work is done by the papers, water and sun. All that the human log-maker has to do is to fold about five newspapers horizontally, and place them inside a full-sized seed tray with no drainage holes – or any other similarly shaped container into which they will fit. While pressing them down, fill the tray with water until the newspapers are submerged and have stopped bubbling. After a short time (just a few minutes – though they can be left for longer) they will be saturated.

Remove a folded, soaked paper and, with the fold on the left, roll it up moderately tightly. Take a second folded newspaper and, with the fold on the right, roll this one round the first roll. Putting the folded end first on the left and then on the right produces a sturdier, more even log. Continue doing this until the Swiss-roll-ish newspapers are the right size to push into the Log Maker. Now follow the instructions for pressing down and squeezing out the water. I stand on the Log Maker for a few seconds until the water has stopped oozing. Remove the 'log' and put it somewhere where it can drain, stay sheltered from rain and dry out in the sun. The logs are ready when they are lightweight. Squirrel them away for the fire-burning months. These building-brick-sized logs, approximately 9 x 4 x 3in (23 x 10 x 7.5cm), take about five minutes to make but will burn for an hour.

Remedies

Procrastination Before doing something unpleasant – for instance, filling in income-tax forms or ironing shirts – take a few minutes to examine an individual plant. The eyes will be refreshed, something new will enter the mind and the disliked work will become less onerous. Gardening is also a good remedy for those who are apt to be glued to the past. There is very little time for the past in gardening – it is a present-tense occupation, the future contained within it.

Crossness If you do not feel your usual charming self, repeat the procrastination remedy, but for a bit longer, depending on the degree of crossness, which after a short time disappears. If it doesn't, do some gardening. I have tested this and have been assured by friends and relations that it works – though how the plants feel afterwards is another matter.

Tiredness When feeling tired or listless, do a little gardening, indoor or out: it revives the weary and seems to produce energy. I am in no doubt that there is something healing about working with plants. They restore equilibrium and peacefulness (see note on horticultural therapy, page 159). Is there any other activity that, in return for a little time and attention, gives back so much?

Runner bean watch

The bean 'heads' are slowly rising now, becoming vertical after only eight days. (Although they resemble 'heads', they are the original beans, but much bigger now after having absorbed water.) Anchored by the invisible root inside the soil, the neck-like stems force their way out between the opening bean. The stems are thick, sturdy and sappy, unlike other seedling stems.

After a few more days the seed coats that covered and protected, but which are now too small to fit the swollen 'head', wrinkle and drop off like discarded sunhats. Only a few days ago the 'sunhats' were tough, shiny and resilient.

Two days later: the stem is growing taller and with it, on either side, two plump 'arm' leaves, which are not leaves but larders that will eventually shrivel and drop off. They contain all the nourishment needed for this stage in a bean's life.

Salad seeds' germination diary

21 June On the morning of the longest day, I sowed some cut-and-come-again-salad leaves in a flowerpot base 3¼in (8cm) deep by 12in (30cm) in diameter in which I had made a few drainage holes.
23 June, p.m. Pinhead-size spots of green are visible on the soil after only a matter of hours.
Place the pot somewhere you pass frequently so that you can keep an eye on this germination drama and jot down what happens. It is most enjoyable to go outside to check on the seeds and then come inside and continue writing their diary – it makes me feel like a horticultural Boswell.

24 June, a.m. The pinheads have already divided into two oval shapes.
24 June, 2 p.m. The leaves are now revealing the minuscule white stems to which they are attached.
The arrival of these green specks has caused upheavals in the soil, as though something beneath it is heaving it up – which it is. One can almost see the specks grow. This is only a slight exaggeration.
It is astonishing that something that can only be measured in millimetres is so strong.
Question: what provides a huge amount of pleasure yet costs almost nothing? Answer: a packet of 2,000 vegetable seeds (who does the counting?), price 90p. The thin little seed packet contains expectation, potential, excitement, interest, and pleases four of the six senses.
26 June Now a central leaf vein is visible. With their two leaves stretched out horizontally (perfect 'tables' for raindrops to balance on) the seedlings resemble a troupe of miniature athletes, exercising.
It is just as interesting and exciting to watch a seed germinating as it is to see the plant at the height of its maturity and beauty.
I look forward to getting up and seeing what has happened during the night and moonlight.
27 June A bit of squabbling is taking place; the seedlings are pushing each other aside, trying to reach light and space. They resemble rush hour on the underground.
The horizontal leaves are now growing upwards, like palms about to applaud.
29 June The leaves are thickening.
30 June, a.m. Barely visible, except through a magnifying glass, between the two outstretched leaves is a third growth, of what must be the beginning of the third leaf.
30 June, p.m. The potential third leaf is beautifully folded. Plants are the very best of packers; nothing could be gift wrapped more perfectly than the flower of the salad pea (*Pisum sativum*).
The surface of the youngest leaf feels like down or velvet. Does this softness help it to slide between the parent leaves?
1 July, 7 a.m. The tips of the two outer leaves have developed heart-shaped dips. The third leaf's velvety surface is disappearing as it

grows, though it is still small enough to measure on half a centimetre of ruler.

2 July, a.m. The still folded third leaf is now taller and larger than its parent leaves. What was once smooth edged is now deckle edged.

2 July, p.m. The almost heart-shaped parent leaves are now dwarfed by their deckle edged offspring, rather like human families.

7 July The adolescent seedlings have now become a miniature bright green copse through which it must be delightful for creatures such as beetles and ladybirds to amble.

Now the first deckle-edged leaf has appeared, others follow quickly, while the parent leaves stretch out almost horizontally, launched into becoming fully fledged lettuce.

Different seeds germinate in different ways. For instance, spinach emerges with its neck bent and looped, the seed head in the ground. If you are unable to keep animals, the next best thing is to sow seeds and look after the plants. You will feel quite different about seeds you have sown and looked after rather than something bought at a garden centre.

Cooking

When the time comes to take a bowl and knife and cut a selection of perpetual spinach, Swiss chard and pak choi, it seems almost unbelievable, when remembering the seeds rattling in their packets just a couple of months ago.

Before harvesting, bring three pots of water to the boil. Never let freshly picked vegetables wait for water to boil. Let the water wait for the vegetables, for it is more accustomed to waiting between rocks and in streams. For this first tasting, at least, cook – or rather blanch – each vegetable separately; avoid a muddle of flavours. If chemical pesticides haven't been used there's no need to wash the vegetables; the boiling water will do that. Don't dilly-dally between picking and cooking (i.e. no telephone calls). And the last 'don't': don't add salt.

Lower the leaves into the gently bubbling water and, as soon as they turn an even more brilliant green, lift them out with a strainer. This first tasting needs no butter, oil, salt or pepper. It is sufficiently delicious naked, uncontaminated by other distracting flavours. For instance, if salt is added to Swiss chard its slightly sea-ish taste is masked.

The first of the dwarf French beans should also be ready to eat. Snip them off with scissors or a knife rather than fingertips, as this causes less damage. There is no need to top, tail or string them. Again, don't add salt and don't cover the pan or their loud popping won't be heard. When the popping stops – after about three minutes – scoop out and eat. There is a particular sweetness about just-picked beans.

Since writing this, I have become very keen on steaming and now much prefer it to boiling. Vegetables can be semi-steamed, which leaves them with more texture.

The natural sweetness in vegetables and fruit (particularly that of melons) is always surprising. From where does it come? It is worth remembering that fruit and vegetables also contain the 'taste' of the different weather they have encountered: spring and midsummer sunshine, a variety of rains, frost and slithers of lightning. (There was a distinct taste of hail in a wine I once drank whose grapes had been bombarded by strong storms.)

Seeds to sow now, outdoors

Chicory 'Sugar Loaf'
Pak choi 'Canton Dwarf' and 'Joi Choi' F_1 – or sow in August
Scarole 'Cornet de Bordeaux'
Plant saffron (*Crocus sativus*) corms

WHAT TO EAT NOW

Clotted cream and saffron ice cream

¼ pint (150ml) double cream (not too thick, pourable)

Small pinch of saffron (about twenty strands; a large pinch will give a bitter taste)

2 egg yolks

1½–2oz (40–50g) vanilla sugar (less sweet is preferable, allowing the saffron to have prominence)

Pinch of salt

¼ pint (150ml) clotted cream

Place the double cream and saffron in a saucepan over a moderate heat an bring to boiling point. With a wooden spoon beat together the yolks, suga and pinch of salt. Pour this mixture into the heated cream and stir until the back of the spoon becomes coated. Do not boil or the mixture will separate. Remove from the heat and leave until cold, stirring occasionally to prevent a skin from forming. Fold the clotted cream into the custard. Pour this mixture into an ice-cream maker. If not using one, pour into a sturdy polythene container and cover with a lid. When the mixture is partially frozen, stir with a fork until smooth and refreeze until firm.

PREVIOUS PAGE Cat nap in scented garden.

Below Aerial view of garden, pigeon, table and chairs.
Bottom left Pigeon inspecting figs, watched by stone nude.
Bottom right Bedroom window with tomato plant 'curtains'.
Right above Door on to roof garden.
Right below Rear view, smothered in honeysuckle, runner beans and jasmine.

PREVIOUS PAGES **Left, clockwise from top left** Germination; door on to roof garden, showing cat's flap and gardening galoshes; harvesting salad on dining-room table. **Right** Roof garden seen through dining-room window.

This page, clockwise from top left Pigeon guarding Bird Café; figs ripening; Conference pears; strawberries; Victoria plums.
Opposite page, clockwise from top left Mixed leaf salad; tomatoes; sweet corn; courgette; herb harvest of dill, mint, and basil; harvest of tomatoes, beans, cucumber, Maori and Scottish potatoes and plums; cat's grass 'lawn'; spinach germinating.

CAT'S LAWN
7.6.10

Clockwise from top right
So-called weed bouquet; jasmine (*Trachelospermum jasminoides*); salad flower; geraniums; Cretan flowers; salad flowers.

July

Plants as presents

Don't imagine that when you generously offer friends hand-sown, hand-reared tomato, basil or cucumber plants they will be accepted with open arms. Sometimes they will, but quite often they won't. Friends of the latter variety will politely shy away, saying that they a) have not enough room (they often have twice the size of your own accommodation), b) have not enough time (even though you remind them that they are tomatoes you are offering, not armadillos or some other alarming foreign pet), or c) can't take the responsibility (as though they are being asked to foster a bunch of delinquent children). Lack of green fingers is another reason, despite your suggestion that this might well be remedied by a season of looking after a tomato or two; in fact, they might possibly enjoy the experience. In the end you may have to beg a friend to foster a few plants, guaranteeing step-by-step plant-rearing tuition by telephone, in return for their generosity. Ah well . . . never mind. Some of the most rewarding recipients of plants are *Big Issue* sellers.

Travelling with seeds and plants[1]

Once you start sowing and growing seeds and plants you will discover new interests when you are away and new places to go away to. For example, when abroad, I always look in the potato department of supermarkets, street markets and greengrocers to see if there are any potatoes I haven't encountered before. From Paris I returned with some purple potatoes; from New Zealand with some black Maori potatoes; from Zurich with potatoes specially suitable for making rösti. From a

1 Before returning to the UK with any plants, it is wise to consult the RHS.

street market in Marseille came a potted magenta bougainvillea and its clashing red companion. In a meadow on the outskirts of Beijing (not the sort of country one associates with meadows) where I was having a picnic, sitting next to me was an intriguing dried seed head, its seeds already beautifully packed in their pod for transporting back to England. From Cairo came the pips of a small, thin-skinned but intense lemon. From Istanbul a couple of stocky tulip bulbs. From Spain a pot of flowering saffron corms so intense, exotic and erotic I was surprised I was not apprehended at the customs. While visiting France I was almost tempted to bring back a potted evergreen oak sapling, beneath which black truffles like to grow. Fortunately I came to my senses (or what's left of them) and decided that a minute dark garden in central London might possibly not be the ideal place to start a truffle plantation.

Some of the seed travelling companions I return home with and enjoy most are the ones whose identity remains a mystery until they germinate. Even then they can continue to remain anonymous, despite taking them on identification trips to the Chelsea Physic Garden and the Royal Botanic Gardens, Kew, or sending them, carefully wrapped in cotton wool and cling film (the next best thing to an ambulance), to the Royal Horticultural Society.

I always wonder why it is so important for us to know the name of a plant, animal or bird, even though that name is man-made. When I went on a first and last bird-watching trip, we all trudged along a path, the 'birders' dressed in their rather odd bird-watching clothes, weighed down by binoculars, tripods, picnics, cameras and bird-identity books. When the bird they were looking for was spotted (miles away, it seemed to me) tripods were clicked into position, cameras aimed, bird books opened at the right page and finally the bird identified and ticked. More time was spent doing this than looking, so it was more like a shoot, the bird being bagged rather than watched.

An interest in sowing and growing plants also opens up different possibilities of places to travel to. Top of my list would be Peru, for the potato museum in Lima, plus all the Indian potato markets. Although I have been to Spain to see a saffron harvest, I should also like to go to Persia, Greece and Morocco to see how their propagation and harvesting methods differ.

Lastly, there is the pleasure of looking out for particular plants or seeds which you know particular friends like, or being given plants or seeds by friends who know of one's specific interest.

Early one year I was given a giant Greek single garlic clove, 2ft (60 cm) high and 2½ft (75cm) wide, whose original home is in Tinos, a small Cycladic island. Before planting it, I put it outside to wait for weather more akin to the Cyclades than the Arctic. But the impatient garlic couldn't wait and although it had just been laid casually on a seed tray, its roots were soon gripping at the earth, longing to get into it, while its tip sprouted a pale green shoot.

Beijing bean

The other side of the plants-as-presents coin is seen in the case of the Beijing bean. While having a late autumn Chinese picnic on the outskirts of Beijing, I picked up a few pods and seed heads, having no idea (at this stage in their life) what they were. On returning home, I gave one of the pods to a friend at the Battersea Park Horticultural Therapy (now renamed Thrive) centre where I work as a volunteer. Several months later, both pod and picnic forgotten, my friend presented me with a small plant in a small pot. It had furry, ivy-shaped leaves and great potential for growing and twining. A short time after it had been repotted, it produced several blue, miniature, morning-glory-like flowers whose buds are also furry – more like small birds than buds.

The flowers are wide awake in the early morning (having succeeded in adjusting to the time difference), then close promptly at about midday – half-day-closing flowers. When they die they leave behind what look like plump, pincushion-shaped fruits, held by five furry, elegantly designed claws. (How often the number five occurs in the plant world, in the number of petals and the shape of leaves. I am not numerologically inclined, but have always regarded five as a good number because of our five fingers and toes; the frequent presence of the number five in plants reinforces this choice.)

This Beijing bean, given as a seed pod and then returned as a plant, is the source of great pleasure and interest. In a few weeks it will be taken on an excursion to Kew to be identified. One of its cousins now lives near Bristol. I should very much like to be given seeds from a country to which I have never been. It makes travelling even more interesting. It might be better to spend time collecting a few seeds than wasting it taking photographs that you and your friends will probably never want to look at.

In praise of Italian rocket

Rocket – I use *rucola coltivata* (produced by Franchi seeds) – must be one of the best seeds for a seed-sowing novice. Even the most anxious or impatient of beginners would be delighted by the speed of its germination. Only three days after sowing it, there were green specks on the surface of the compost. A day later a team of anaemic, spindly-stemmed seedlings were pushing their way upwards towards the light, raising the compost as they did so.

Confession number three, concerning miniature root vegetables

I have had little or, to be honest, no success with these vegetables and I have grown quite a few of them: carrots, celeriac, fennel, turnips and spring onions. A few months ago I had a final fling with beetroot. I don't know why I keep trying as I rather despise these stunted, so-called vegetables, which are only really for people with blasé palates. What is the point of eating something which is almost dimensionless? In their way they are as pointless as their malformed, generally tasteless giant equivalents.

They are not difficult to germinate. In the case of dolls' house beetroot, highly polished, dark-Burgundy-verging-on-chocolate leaves soon appear, their maroon phosphorescent stems already bleeding vivid blood-red sap. However, below ground virtually nothing in the way of growth takes place, either horizontally or vertically. The pygmy beetroots just sit there for months on end pretending to be a table decoration, the leaves becoming tougher and rougher, not even suitable for salad.

Despite giving them such a damning report, I will definitely try growing them again next year.

Feeding

Feeding the vegetables begins when their flowers turn into fruits – tomatoes, cucumbers and aubergines, for instance – or, in the case of salad vegetables, when they reach the adolescent stage. Apart from the pelletized organic chicken manure added when filling the containers with soil (see page 42), a little more sustenance can be given now, plus some extract of seaweed (half a capful in 2 gallons or 9 litres of water). As most of this will drain away, another alternative (though both may be employed) is to foliar feed. This requires a small container, called a hose-end feeder (available from garden centres), which is attached to the end of the hose and filled with the seaweed extract. Water and feed are then mixed in the right proportions and sprayed on the leaves. Avoid windy days, strong sunshine and when it is about to rain; also avoid spraying when the beans are starting to flower, for they are too fragile to withstand the weight of the falling droplets. This form of feeding leaves gives a pleasant, seaside-ish sort of smell, intriguing in the centre of a city.

This may be wishful thinking, but there was a definite difference in taste between the seaweed/pelletized manure-fed tomatoes and those fed with a much-advertised chemical feed.

Beans

The runner beans have started to bloom in red. Some of the flowers have already begun to turn into beans. Don't wait until they are boomerang shaped before picking or they will be furry, stringy and tough. Pick when a little bigger than a dwarf French bean, about 4–5in (10–12cm) long.

Most window-boxes, pots and tubs can have a runner bean or two planted inside them. They clamber and scramble up everything even vaguely vertical: wisteria, plum and pear trees, drainpipes, honeysuckle, washing lines and jasmine. As they are quite chameleon-ish, this makes harvesting them a game of hide-and-seek between the leaves.

One of their favourite supports is a *Viburnum* x *burkwoodii* that is now the size of a little tree. A non-gardening friend spotted the beans hanging from the viburnum branches and asked what the plant was. '*Vibeanum* x *burkwoodii*,' I explained to my credulous friend. Also using the viburnum climbing frame is a cucumber.

Bean and alpine strawberry diary

It is worthwhile jotting down how runner bean flower buds become edible beans. At the same time write an alpine strawberry diary.

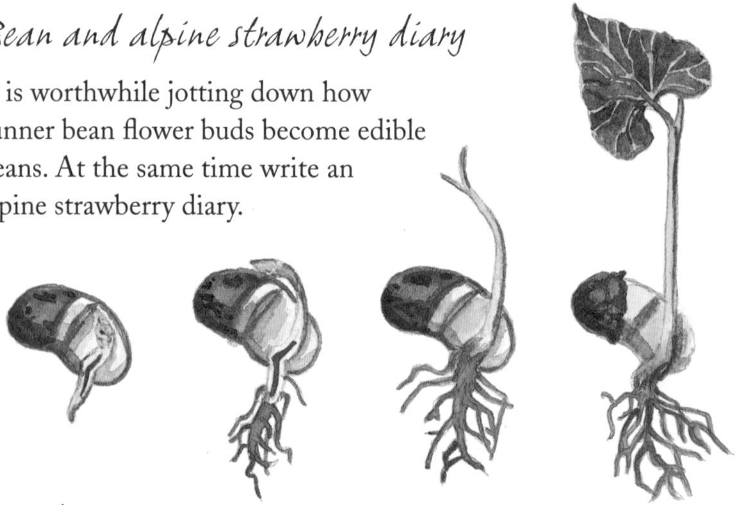

6 July Tie a piece of soft twine round the bean stem which is to be observed. Green bud is as small as a risotto rice grain; no hint of the flower's redness to come.
First alpine strawberry in flower.
7 July, 8.45 a.m. Bean bud slightly larger. Red is entering the green, producing a greeny-orange colour.
8 July Green tinge disappearing, bean bud plumping out into two fat, little puffed-out cheeks.
Alpine strawberry petals have fallen, leaving a pointed, pitted-thimble, off-white fruit.
11 July Bean still swelling.
12 July Bean swelling completed. During the night the puffed-out cheeks opened, revealing a snapdragon-ish flower inside.

And so on . . .

It would be disgraceful to be asked at the end of one's life how a bean-flower bud becomes a bean and not to know the answer. How many summers has one been witness to this so-called common-or-garden event without ever really having seen it happen?

Common or garden

The *Oxford English Dictionary* definition: 'passing into adj., in the slang phr. common or garden, a jocular substitute for "common", "ordinary"'.

So-called pests

Don't worry about them. People who concentrate on pests fail to see the plants on which they perch. Insects, like so-called weeds, and we must be on this earth for a reason, not just plonked here arbitrarily. There are only two 'pest' antidotes I use. The first is an organic insecticidal soap spray (it can be obtained on the Internet, under the unpleasant name of Bio Pest Pistol), which to date has only been used against blackfly on nasturtiums and against scale on an orange bush. It can also be used against whitefly, greenfly and red spider mite; if used properly, it does not harm ladybirds. The second is a children's library book on insects. I consulted this when a group of yellow, caviar-sized balls gathered together (like a circular bus queue) on the back of a nasturtium leaf. Thinking they might be another form of black- or greenfly, I was about to aim the only too easy-to-use Pistol at them, but decided to return to the children's library and re-borrow the book on insects. The yellow 'caviar' turned out to be butterfly eggs, laid on a nasturtium instead of a cabbage leaf. What happened next took place in August: see page 92.

Perfect-lawn mania is another aspect of horticulture with which gardeners are apt to become afflicted, failing to see the lawn for the 'weeds' and molehills. After all, a lawn is only an unnaturally cultivated, comparatively dull crew-cut stretch of Wilton carpet, which is presumably for lying and walking on. If its 'owner' becomes demented by the natural appearance of a few daisies and dandelions and by the grass's constant demand to be mowed, what is the point of it? Where is the pleasure? Trying to force something to behave in a way in which it was never intended seems a somewhat fruitless exercise. I would not care to be the child of an obsessive lawn owner.

Small trays versus containers

The advantages of sowing seeds in small 8 x 6in (20 x 15cm) trays instead of directly into containers are that it is easier to see what you and the seeds (both before and after germination) are doing, and there is more to observe. The seedlings receive individual attention. The trays can be moved round to follow the sun or find the shade. (This can of course be done at all stages of window-box gardening.)

If you are going away for the weekend by car, and have no one to do the watering, you could take the trays with you. If they would be unwelcome, then before leaving get a small plastic bottle, fill it with water, cover the open end with your thumb, turn the bottle upside down and quickly submerge it in the compost.

To plant the trays, follow the seed-sowing instructions on pages 7–8, up to and including stage 5, until the compost has drained. Divide the tray into four lengthways with a pencil, laying it on the compost and pushing it to and fro while pressing down and creating a furrow. Then, depending on the size of the seed, deepen the furrow with the crab march (i.e. by marching your four fingertips sideways up and down, making little mounds on either side: see page 59). Write the name of seed, the date and, if large enough, the number of seeds sown. Unless the seeds are very small they can be sown individually, or trickled slowly into the furrows. Then with your forefingers return the mounds, covering the seeds. A 9in (23cm) long furrow full of seeds will be sufficient to stock a 28 x 8 x 8in (70 x 20 x 20cm) window-box.

A recent discovery

Cut-and-come-again salads are perfectly content growing in much smaller and shallower containers than I previously used, making it possible for people to grow them with even less space than I have. At the moment fifteen different salads are growing in saucers measuring anything from 12–8in (30–20cm) in diameter and between 3–2in (7–5cm) deep. Filled window-boxes or deep tubs are both heavy and cumbersome to move, whereas smallish saucers are portable. For those in favour of a dining-table épergne, what could be more original and attractive than an edible centrepiece saucer of mixed salad? Harvesting the saucer salads, either leaf by leaf or trimming with scissors, makes one feel like an apprentice hairdresser.

Another advantage of the portability of saucers is that it makes it much easier to observe germination. It is surprising how dramatic and exciting it is to watch a lettuce seed, the size of a pencil tip, germinating. It is well worth writing a diary of its progress.

P.S. To make drainage holes in the plastic salad saucers, heat the end of a sturdy screwdriver on a gas or electric cooker plate. Being careful that it doesn't slip, pierce the bottom of the saucers with several evenly spaced holes.

Will the future be flowerless?

Just because you concentrate on vegetables and fruit this does not mean a flowerless future, for – much to some people's surprise – fruits, vegetables and herbs also have flowers. They may not be as buxom and fluorescent as the flowers we are accustomed to; they just need to be discovered and looked at differently.

Vegetable flowers

Instead of pulling up vegetables that are about to bolt (run to seed prematurely), let them bolt and then cut them as flowers. The world of vegetable flowers is not really appreciated; they are not given a chance to bloom. So now is the time to let them complete their cycle and examine them properly.

For instance rocket, whose leaves are by now singeing the mouth, has little pale buff-coloured, complicated, propeller flowers: old fashioned, intricate, strange – as though from the nether world. It is a somewhat mysterious, almost creepy flower one wouldn't quite trust, unlike an open-faced daisy. It is the sort of flower a medieval German artist might have engraved. Despite this, it will sit happily in a vase for several days. Pak choi has gentle, yellow countryside-scent flowers of which the eaters of stir-fries know nothing. White basil flowers, despite their smallness, smell (not unnaturally) strongly of basil. They are snapdragon-ish in form, having a bouncy platform (or, if seen in profile, what resembles a Habsburg lip) on which small insects can land and stand while feeding.

Seeds to sow now, outdoors

Winter purslane

WHAT TO EAT NOW

'Gardener's Delight' tomatoes

This is a combination of small sweet 'Gardener's Delight' tomatoes, hummus, black olives and a tin of tuna fish in olive oil.

August

5.45 a.m. roof-garden visit

The silence that surrounds and emanates from plants is intense: it is not only oxygen and carbon dioxide that they emit.

Whether or not to talk to plants

Not – at least out loud; there's no need to. We do quite enough chattering as it is. As silence is one of the most remarkable of plant qualities (from which we might learn), they probably prefer silent communication. Plants either do or do not sense the feelings of the person tending them. But if bread and mayonnaise are affected by the cook's mood, then it seems likely that plants will be too. As in the case of wheat, yeast, oil and eggs, it is through the hands that 'communication' probably takes place.

A vivid example of silence is present at the Chelsea Flower Show. Apart from the plants' beauty and scent, also striking is their stillness and silence when surrounded by the uproar of constantly talking and moving *Homo sapiens*.

Market gardens

Another advantage of growing vegetables in small trays is that they can be held up to the light to see which of the seedling silhouettes need thinning. If you are short of space, another method of extending the 'allotment' is to ask a greengrocer for some plastic mushroom-transporting boxes. These are about 15 x 11 x 3½in (38 x 28 x 9cm), are generally green or blue and are not too hideous, even though they are plastic. They already have holes in them to aerate the mushrooms; in fact, there are so many holes that the boxes will need to be lined. Woven imitation hessian sacks (made of polypropylene and the same as those used for lining the château wormery: see pages 120 and 171, K) cut to the right size are ideal. Whatever you use, make certain there are sufficient holes to allow the compost to drain.

Fill the greengrocer's trays with compost. If possible water them from below; if not, lightly from above with a watering can. Divide them into five rows length- or widthwise and prick out the seedlings with the shoehorn dibber. Any spare seedlings can be planted in other comfortable-looking pots – or eaten.

One of my market gardens contains:
1 row of five komatsuna
1 row of five 'Sugar Loaf' chicory
1 row of five Texsel greens
1 row of five Chinese cabbage 'Tah Tsai'
1 row of five mizuna
Total: twenty-five plants

Beetroot 'Detroit 2-Tardel' needs somewhere a little deeper to grow, so it has been put in a window-box. What is going to cause its underground swelling? There is no suggestion of it at the moment; only the bright maroon stems hint at what is to come.

Continuation of the butterfly's yellow eggs story

Most people probably already know this story, but, for those who don't, here it is, similar to the mealworm's (see page 36), but different. I would be happy to be told this drama of metamorphosis as a bedtime story every night.

Metamorphosis

The *Oxford English Dictionary* definition:
'Pl. metamorphoses Brit.
a. The action or process of changing in form, shape, or substance; esp. transformation by supernatural means . . .
3.a. Biol. Change of form in an animal (or plant), or its parts, during post-embryonic development; spec. the process of transformation from an immature form to a different adult form that many insects and other invertebrates, and some vertebrates (e.g. frogs), undergo in the course of maturing.'

The butterfly that laid the eggs was probably a cabbage white. After mating for two hours, the male butterfly flies away and the female finds a place to lay her eggs. As central London is not overrun with cabbage patches, a nasturtium leaf was chosen. After laying her eggs, she dies.

Egg

The *Oxford English Dictionary* definition: 'The (more or less) spheroidal body produced by the female of birds and other animal species and containing the germ of a new individual, enclosed within a shell or firm membrane.'

Surrounding the eggs is a substance that sticks them to the leaf. Inside each egg a caterpillar is growing. After about ten days it will hatch via a little hole through which it nibbles its way out. It is now a larva.

Larva

The *Oxford English Dictionary* definition: 'Pl. larvae. Latin *larva* a ghost, spectre, hobgoblin; also, a mask. An insect in the grub state, i.e. from the time of its leaving the egg till its transformation into a pupa.'

'So in his silken sepulchre the worm, warm'd with
new life, unfolds his larva-form.'
Erasmus Darwin (1731–1802)

With sharp jaws, the ravenous baby 'hobgoblin' caterpillar eats the rest of the empty eggshell before starting on the leaf. As it devotes all its time to eating, it grows quickly until it resembles a long, stiff-haired dachshund. Its skin soon becomes too tight and starts to split. It changes skins (each a larger size) four times. When three weeks have passed it will be fully grown, having reached the halfway stage. It is now a pupa.

Pupa

The *Oxford English Dictionary* definition:
'Plural pupae Brit. 1.a. Entomol. In insects that
undergo complete metamorphosis: a stage in the life
cycle that is transitional between larva and adult, and
which is typically a quiescent resting phase; (also) an
insect in this stage; a chrysalis.'

The 'nymph doll' now stops eating and crawls away to find a safe place. Before settling down, it spins a silk thread that comes from a hole just below the mouth. The silk forms a bed for it to lie on and attaches it to its new resting place. Now another strange event takes place: the fourth and last skin splits. Inside is a soft chrysalis. After a few hours it hardens, still attached by the silk-thread guy ropes. What intriguing, almost secretive words are employed in this whole process.

Chrysalis

The *Oxford English Dictionary* definition:
'Pl. chrysalides or chrysalises but chrysalids is often
substituted; cf. orchids. Latin *chrysallis*, *chrysalis*, Greek . . .
"The gold-coloured sheath of butterflies", deriv. of . . . "gold".
1. The state into which the larva of most insects passes
before becoming an imago or perfect insect.
In this state the insect is inactive and takes no food,
and is wrapped in a hard sheath or case.'

The chrysalis remains on its silk bed for weeks and sometimes months while inside it a wingless caterpillar begins to change into a winged butterfly. Through the transparent chrysalis case the spots on the future butterfly's wings can sometimes be seen – that is, if it is going to be a female cabbage white. Males have no spots.

When the time is right the butterfly slowly pushes its way out of the case until it splits. When it finally emerges it rests on the empty case, its wings crumpled, damp and slowly unfolding.

After about an hour the wings will have become the right shape, though they are still soft and damp, not ready for flight. After two more hours have passed, the wings will be dry: the butterfly is ready to fly. The imago is complete.

Imago

The *Oxford English Dictionary* definition: 'Plural imagines, US imagos . . . Entomol. The final or adult stage in the development of an insect, during which it is sexually mature.'

This extraordinary creature, which is two creatures in one, now has a complete change of food, from spicy-savoury to sweet. No longer will it search for cabbage and nasturtium leaves to nibble, but for nectar to sip, its hollow tongue (which can be extended or retracted) being used as a straw.

Nectar

The *Oxford English Dictionary* definition:
'Etymology: < classical Latin *nectar* the drink of the gods, wine or other sweet drink, . . . fluid containing fructose, glucose, and other sugars that is secreted by the nectaries of plants, esp. to attract pollinators.'

'Sweet Honey some condense . . .
The rest, in Cells apart, the liquid Nectar shut.'
John Dryden (1631–1700), *Georgics*, Book iv

Soon the butterfly will mate and the circle will be completed, ready to begin again.

To know this story should make people think twice, if not thrice, before killing a caterpillar. Are not butterflies preferable to cabbages?

More so-called pests and insects

As caterpillars proved to be so unexpectedly absorbing, I thought I might as well get to know some of the other window-box creatures; there is bound to be some assistant-gardener insect observing one's activities. To know just the minimum amount transforms them from enemies into what they are: extraordinary insects. For example, the so-called common wasp is probably the greatest of the insect architects and builders. Using chewed wood pulp, which turns into paper, it builds its spherical Baroque-style nest. Its colleague the potter wasp uses soft mud when constructing its jar-shaped nest.

Another favourite insect is the furry, striped, wasp imitator, the stingless hoverfly. It can remain motionless, suspended in mid-air or, with the acceleration of a sports car, fly backwards, forwards or sideways, even when it is windy.

Woodlice are more interesting than they appear. They 'wear' their skeletons, called exoskeletons, on the outside of their bodies.

Snails are also not only to be looked down upon. Their slow-motion mating is enviably sensuous.

If you have made yourself a small pond (for instructions see pages 55–6), you might encounter gnats. They will become less irritating when you know that they lay their eggs on the surface of the water in groups which resemble a raft. When the larvae hatch, they hang upside down in the water, breathing air through a siphon. (*Mycetophila fungorum* gnats emit a light, not to assist fellow gnats in finding their way but to lure other insects into their silken traps.)

There are more different species of insect than all the different kinds of mammals, fish, birds and reptiles put together – well over a million. However, the reader of this book will be relieved to know that, for the time being, only two freshwater favourites will be mentioned.

The water boatman swims on its back under water using its flattened hind legs as oars. When it needs to breathe it rises to the surface, collects a bubble of air under its wings and descends, like a diver using an oxygen tank. Water boatmen that swim on their fronts are for some odd reason called lesser water boatmen. Why should this method of swimming make them lesser?

The pond skater is so light in weight it can walk on water without sinking. (On the top of still freshwater there is a mysterious 'skin', called 'surface tension', which prevents lightweight objects from sinking.) Despite the near biblical feat of walking on water, its large eyes look rather melancholy.

When you know that insects, like us, have heads, eyes, legs, lungs, hearts, feet, abdomen, nerves, thorax and guts, you will feel less inclined to crush them underfoot.

Returning to the pond

It is worth having a pond if only to provide a drinking trough for visiting insects, some of which are supposed to be able to smell a pond's existence from 2 miles (3km) away. So far no dragonflies have been alerted to my pond's presence, though wasps and hoverflies (which are ½in/10mm long and have a similar, but paler, uniform to wasps' with one pair of wings instead of two) make up for their absence. Balancing on the pygmy lily pads, with their cargoes of dew, these miniature tigers – heads lowered, striped posteriors throbbing – sip. A much smaller pond insect (back to the children's library to find its name) skates across the water leaving no footprints on the mysterious surface tension.

In this quite different world of aquatic plants, it is astonishing that buds, leaves and stems can not only survive but develop under water before flowering above it. Young lily pads spend quite a time sulking beneath the surface. Why don't they rot? Of what sort of 'mackintosh material' are these underwater plants constituted? At least ponds should cause their own owners to wonder.

Depending on when the pond was installed and whether or not it has a pygmy waterlily, at some time during the growing season, after the lily's pads have ascended to the surface, it may need a little nourishment. This comes in the shape of a Café Noir biscuit-sized tablet which, when the pygmy has been hauled up from the 9in (23cm) depths, is slipped into its growing basket. While doing this I also added an oxygenator called *Elodea crispa*, given to me by a pond friend in exchange for a yoghurt carton of floating beaver. I would infinitely prefer to be given something from a friend's pond than a bottle of Lambrusco or a box of After Eights. Another advantage: pond presents or swaps are easy to transport.

Potato, alpine strawberry, cucumber, pear, beetroot, plum, artichoke, cherry, nasturtium and tomato report

The 8in (20cm) pots of potatoes will now be filled to within 1in (2.5cm) of their tops and sprouting huge bouquets of stems (called haulms), leaves and perhaps flowers. When they have flowered or begin to show signs of wilting, it is time to see what is going on beneath the soil. First, make certain it is not too dry or too wet, but just right. Second, holding the haulms by the scruff of their necks, close to the soil, gently ease both soil and haulms out of the pot. Embedded in the soil, but just visible, should be new potatoes. Third, disturbing the soil as little as possible, carefully remove one potato, and then return everything to the pot, giving it a little shake to fill the potato-less hollow. Now that the potatoes' presence has been confirmed, next time you repeat this procedure, make certain that a pot of water is boiling before delving inside the pot.

Alpine strawberries (sown early in the year) are still flowering and fruiting in their hanging basket. Wait until they are dark red before picking; their scent is more intense at this stage.

Slicing the cucumber completes the seed-sowing circle, for there, in the sap-oozing slice, are the sculling-boat-shaped seeds ready for next season's sowing. There are thirteen of them. Hidden inside the cucumber is a seed mandala – an archetypal design.

The solitary 'Comice' pear continues to fatten.

Beetroot, sown on 12 July. Quite often curiosity wins over prudence and I dig up a beetroot plant (as though transplanting it, giving its stem a wide berth and disturbing the roots as little as possible) just to see what's happening underground. I then put it back as if nothing has taken place. If someone would make transparent window-boxes and pots there would be no need to do this. The result of this prying is the realization that the beetroots are only just starting to swell – and that their maroon colour stretches right down to their roots, which are a dark pink.

The 'Victoria' plums are becoming heavier, filling with juice. Is sap related to juice? There are thirty-nine plums.

The Waitrose Jerusalem artichoke, planted on 2 April in a 7in (18cm) tall x 9in (23cm) diameter pot, seems to have mistaken itself for Jack's beanstalk. It is now almost 6ft (1.8m) tall and still growing its bristly, pre-shaven stem and leaves, with no imminent intention to flower. Following the potato examination instructions, you may find, tucked secretly inside its soil, some small artichokes. Remove only those that are to be eaten now. As artichokes are nutty and juicy when grated and eaten raw as a salad, ignore the boiling water lecture.

All the cherries have gone, mostly eaten by the birds. Don't worry; it is well worth letting them have their share just to hear them – surely most cities don't suffer from a superabundance of fruiting cherries. I would prefer to have more birds and fewer cherries than vice versa.

Eating nasturtium flowers seems vaguely cannibalistic, though if one's prepared to eat the fruits of the flower this is a bit illogical. Flowers used as decoration seem a silly, de trop addition. Vegetables are sufficiently attractive in themselves; they don't need decorating.

However, when the nasturtiums finish flowering they leave behind pods that can be made into alternative capers by preserving them in vinegar – something one might do once but probably not twice, unless capers were suddenly unavailable.

Waiting for tomatoes to ripen can be a mysterious process at times.

There they are, hanging on their stems, week after week, plump and green, but with not a hint of changing colour. Days of sunshine beam on them, but the greenness stubbornly persists until, when your back is turned, one day the ripening begins. What is strange about it is that although the tomatoes inhabit different pots and window-boxes they all start ripening at once, as though a tomato-ripening conductor has waved a baton. Included in this ripening mystery are some American (Amish) 'Brandywine' tomatoes, the seeds of which were given to me by a friend. I couldn't resist sowing them, though with reluctance, when I read that they are considered to be the 'best tasting and some of the biggest tomatoes in the world'. This ungrateful seed recipient did not like their untomato-ish leaves and vast sumo-wrestler-sized fruits whose skins bruise, scar and split (size twenty tomatoes squeezed into size fourteen skins). Being so vast, they take longer to ripen, remaining an unattractive lingerie pink long after the modest tiny red globes of 'Gardener's Delight' are being eaten. Fruits and vegetables that are the result of greed breeding are not sympathetic. Generally they are so heavy that they exhaust their stems, weighing down and then breaking the side shoots that try to support them, requiring additional twine-and-stake scaffolding. They are the equivalent of cows that have been bred so large that their distorted, painful-looking udders almost sweep the ground.

Plants are generous, producing not only one crop but, in many cases, crop after crop. Why should they be forced into deformity just to satisfy us? Despite my aversion to them, the 'Brandywine' tomatoes battle on. In this instance there is no need to talk to them. They must sense from the way they are touched that they are not favourites.

There are so many tomatoes now that the tops of the tallest are tied to and supported by a washing line. Six 'Gardener's Delight' stand in front of a permanently open window, forming a green net curtain.

Seeds to sow now, outdoors

Abyssinian mustard (also called Texsel greens)
American land cress (likes shade, so most convenient)
Komatsuna (also called mustard spinach)
Lamb's lettuce (*Valerianella locusta*, also called corn salad and mâche)
Mitsuba (also called Japanese parsley)
Mizuna (also called potherb mustard)
New Zealand spinach (*Tetragonia tetragonioides*)
Pak choi 'Canton Dwarf' and 'Joi Choi' F_1
Radish (*Raphanus sativus*) 'Red Meat'
Swiss chard (*Beta vulgaris* Cicla Group)
Winter purslane (also called miner's lettuce, Indian lettuce and claytonia)

WHAT TO EAT NOW

A small portion of alpine strawberry Jersey ice cream

4oz (110g) alpine strawberries
2oz (50g) icing sugar
juice of half a lemon (optional)
juice of half an orange (optional)
¼ pint (150ml) Jersey double cream

With a fork, gently crush (not smash) the strawberries. Add the sugar gradually. It is the taste, texture and scent of the fruit that should be paramount, not Tate and Lyle. Add teaspoon by teaspoon the lemon and orange juices, if using; these emphasize the flavour. Whip the cream until stiff but not rigid. Fold in the fruit. Freeze.

September

Compost confession

If the witch-like brew of compost in the plastic sack (see pages 39–41) has become too lumpy and wet – not quite what you imagined it would be – four things can be done to remedy it. One: be less enthusiastic with the urine treatment. Two: mix in scrunched-up balls – not torn strips – of paper; the scrunching provides more air. Envelopes (but not those with plastic windows) and bank statements are the right size. Three: contrary to most compost rules, there's sunbathing. Open the sack as wide as possible, roll down the edges and, when the sun shines, let the compost bask in it. Four: roll up a *Radio Times*, creating a wick, make a hole in the compost, and then place the 'wick' inside to draw out any excess moisture. (The *Radio Times* is also suitable for wormeries, not because worms listen to the radio, but because the wick remedy helps to dry them out if they become too wet.)

High-density, already-perforated polythene bags can be bought for the sole purpose of making compost. I am not entirely convinced that they work, except at stage two of composting, which is really the resting and final rotting-down period. For stage one, a small manageable-sized plastic dustbin about 16in tall and 15in in diameter (41 x 38cm) with a lid is easier and more effective. Drill ¾in (2cm) holes all round it at about 2in (5cm) intervals, creating an Aertex dustbin. Don't make holes in the top (or rain will get in) and make only a few in the bottom, for drainage. It is much easier to turn a dustbin than a heavy sack – especially if the dustbin has a lid that 'locks'.

More compost ingredient suggestions: wood ash (not coal ash) provides potassium and lime; old woollen (not synthetic) clothes;

the manure and bedding of vegetarian animals (guinea pigs, gerbils and rabbits); ground eggshells (if not being used for a wormery); hair (human and animal) – I only add animal hair (cat combings), human hair being less appealing, but both contain nitrogen. (Some people, particularly spinners and weavers, feel quite friendly towards hair and will collect every available strand. When visiting a weavers' and spinners' annual fair, a weaver pointed to a colleague whose top half was dressed in a dowdy brown, dusty-looking, hand-knitted cardigan. With a mixture of enthusiasm and envy she explained that the cardigan was made of Alsatian dog combings. I imagine the hair had suited the Alsatian better than it did its present owner.)

As more waste is added to the Aertex dustbin, the ingredients become heavier, darker and more unrecognizable.

The reason why plants need nitrogen is somewhat tricky to understand, but without it leaves become yellow. Some of a plant's nitrogen comes from the air, which the bacteria in its roots convert into nitrogen compounds. The most interesting converter of nitrogen is lightning, its searing heat forming nitrogen compounds that dissolve in rain and then wash into the soil.

Paper log harvest

Among the other September crops is the paper log harvest. When the logs have finished drying outside and become lightweight, they are brought inside for a final drying. I lay mine side by side on the steps of a closed ladder. I haven't been particularly diligent in log-making this year, but there are already thirty-one waiting to be burned, which equals about thirty-one hours of sitting in front of the fire. And there is still time to make more.

Wormery disaster no. 1

There has been quite an upheaval in the wormery. Thinking that the worms would be better protected from rain in the 'greenhouse' (i.e. a little structure measuring 41 x 20 x 44in or 104 x 50 x 112cm, the sides, back and top of which are enclosed in clear plastic sheeting), I moved them on to its only shelf to share it with the drying-out 'logs'. They were protected from rain, but not from an unusually warm burst of September weather. The result: cremation – and shame.

'I never . . . trode upon a worme against my will, but I wept for't.'
William Shakespeare (1564–1616), *Pericles*

Wormery disaster no. 2

After being sent a replacement colony of 250 worms by one of the generous suppliers, I moved the wormery back to its original and more clement home beneath the garden table. Thinking that the replacement colony of reds and tigers might like a welcoming treat, I gave them the cat's leftover rather superior tinned food. The 'treat' killed them. Protein poisoning was apparently the culprit. What does it do to cats?

Since then the suppliers of the Can-O-Worms wormery (see page 171, K) have given me one to test. It is a black plastic, circular, four-storey construction (plus lid) on stilts – something between a high-rise borstal and ultra-modern chalet. Although it is not an object of beauty, it does provide a most interesting way of observing worm life. Starting on the ground floor, the worms gradually eat their way up. To do this they have to squeeze through the perforated ceiling-floors. The perforations are only ¼in (5mm) in diameter. At first it was difficult to understand how plump adult worms with ⅓in (8mm) waists were going to squeeze themselves through ¼in (5mm) holes. The suppliers confirmed that the worms would, if there was sufficiently tempting food on the other side of the perforation. And they did, plump worms suddenly elongating themselves into slim, svelte worms. It was through the Can-O-Worms supplier that I discovered the *Worm Digest*, a quarterly American newspaper to which I have not subscribed – yet. It reveals that in North America there are worm symposiums, dinners, galas and tours, videos, conferences (national and international), congresses, CDs (Rot 'n' Roll), consultants (and no doubt counsellors), and worm workshops and networking.

Closing down

Late September is closing-down and closing-up time: barbecues are scrubbed and brought indoors; deck chairs are stacked; garden umbrellas are made vertical, the imprint of summer caught in the bleached folds of canvas; fans are switched off, dust gathering on the motionless propellers. The arm of the barometer moves towards the left. The air indoors and outdoors is different: there is now a divide. Windows that have been left open all summer are closed, almost. Autumn winds cause the trees to heave and the leaves to make a sea-ish sound. Garden doors swell. Bats hibernate. Plants are fed for the last time, and bird feeders are filled. Late autumn-sown seeds germinate slowly. If everything else is doing something quite different, what should we be doing? Not everything is closing down at this time. Events that can't be seen are also taking place, hidden inside apparently dead flower heads. Although they may be brown and brittle, they are still alive. Seeds are fattening, their coats hardening in preparation for winter. One of the most beautiful and astonishing is the geranium seed. When the dried, spiky flower heads are ready to spring open, they reveal a still-closed, feather-like wing or sail, at the base of whose mast is a seed anchor. Everything is prepared for flight, landing and germination.

The report

Wild strawberry plants are looking tired and too relaxed, though they are still producing pointed thimbles of sweetness and scent, but less abundantly.

I am still eating runner and 'Sprite' dwarf beans. If the runners become too big and long, just eat the beans and donate the pods to the worms or compost.

Beijing bean flowers are already open at 5.45 a.m. when it is still darkish – more duskish than dawn. The flowers close at 10.30 a.m.

At the base of the plant, thc pincushion pods are losing their colour, the sap withdrawing, the pods hardening and browning into fragile, wood-like containers.

The bush and sweet basil are just as prolific as ever.

'Fresh basil . . . is too precious for so much as one leaf to be allowed to go to waste.'
Elizabeth David (1913–92), *Summer Cooking*

There are still plenty of 'Gardener's Delight' and 'Brandywine' tomatoes on the vines, enough to give to friends who have forgotten the taste of tomatoes. Apologies, of a sort, are due to the 'Brandywine' tomatoes, one of which weighed 12oz (350g). When sliced and interleaved with basil and mozzarella, sprinkled with lemon and basil-infused oil, it made a vast breadless sandwich. The soupçon-sized 'Gardener's Delight' still remain my first choice.

Two cucumbers are waiting to be picked.

There are plenty of snippings to be made from recently sown leaves. Whether one is or is not supposed to pick young beetroot leaves, they are being picked, each a different colour and pattern and particularly juicy. The salad-leaf-nibbling insects and I have come to a unanimous decision: we don't care for 'Sugar Loaf' chicory or scarole; they are too bitter and the only leaves that the insects ignore. So they won't be sown again, despite chicory's beautifully wrapped conical hearts and the squeaky sound its leaves make.

At last the aubergines have started to flower: the sort of wrinkled, pale lilac, yellow-centred flowers that appear in old Germanic tapestries.

The lavender flowers are now faded and dry, their nectar stored in bees' cells in unknown hives, the flowers collected in bags and scenting the darkness inside wardrobes, instead of the summer air.

Seeds to sow now, outdoors

Abyssinian mustard (also called Texsel greens)
Komatsuna (also called mustard spinach)
Lamb's lettuce (*Valerianella locusta*) – can be sown until April
Radish (*Raphanus sativus*) 'Red Meat' – can be sown until October
Swiss chard (*Beta vulgaris* Cicla Group) – can be sown until mid-September

WHAT TO EAT NOW

Basil butter

Scented herb butters can be made using most herbs, either on their own or by mixing them. As well as basil, both dill and lemon thyme make good butters.

a handful of basil leaves

unsalted butter

lemon juice

pinch of salt

Finely chop the basil leaves, not stems, and mix with the softened, unsalted butter, a drop of lemon juice and a pinch of salt.

October

October gardening

Most Octobers are not particularly tempting months for working outdoors. You have to entice yourself to go out. The sunshine doesn't warm the marrow; it is not for basking in. It is either weak as skimmed milk or brilliant and slanting, painted on but not penetrating, making gardening short and intense.

But there is still quite a lot to be done. Cut the dead or dying tomato plants, beans, cucumbers, basil stalks, the 6ft (1.8m) Jerusalem artichoke into 1in (2.5cm) pieces for the compost to enable it to continue its metamorphosis. The no-longer-green bean stems cling to whatever they have attached themselves to with such strength that they could almost be made into rope ladders – or an alternative to Rapunzel's hair.

Delicate plants, like the orange bush, are brought indoors. So are small pots of parsley and chives.

Seed legacies

A friend, who always emphasized her lack of green fingers, managed to her great satisfaction to grow a pot of Italian flat-leaved parsley on her kitchen windowsill. As she had too many parsley seeds she gave some to me. A few years later she died. I am still growing those seeds. Of the many seed packets I have, these are special. So is each parsley germination . . . or reincarnation – more so than the monetary legacy she kindly left me. Seeds and plants could be left in wills for the sake of both the will-writer and the legatee.

Saffron

This, at last, is the month when the harvesting of the *Crocus sativus* stigmas should take place.

'Thy plants are an orchard of pomegranates,
with pleasant fruits; camphire, with spikenard,
spikenard and saffron . . .'
The Song of Solomon

One late October I went to a Spanish saffron festival in La Mancha and returned with double the quantity of saffron enthusiasm . . . plus a flower pot of *Crocus sativus*, still in leaf, which sits contentedly on my London window ledge. A couple of hours' bus drive from Toledo, in a field beside a road sheltered by grandmotherly olive trees, the rows of crocus grow. From a distance what appears to be a lilac mist hovers low over the ground. Close up, when standing above the flowers, comes the shock of seeing their interiors set alight by orange-red stigma and yellow style. Orange-red, lilac and yellow: one might imagine it would be a gaudy combination. But it is not. The saffron 'farmers' ('crocers' they used to be called when saffron was grown in England) are plucking the flowers, backs bent double, solid boots placed on either side of the rows of heavy, sandy soil, big wicker baskets filling slowly with the weightless harvest. Behind the pluckers a hill rises. Mounting its side sit the silhouettes of seven windmills, sail-less arms saluting the sky. For the festival, the bare windmill arms will be dressed with sails.

In La Mancha, down a narrow street, behind a door, is a yard. At the side of it beneath a tin roof is a space where a cart or car might be parked. But, instead of cart or car, on the ground is a billowing double-bed-sized carpet of thousands of saffron flowers over which intoxicated bees hover. A cloud could have landed. It's impossible not to kneel and bury one's face in the softness of the flowers, inhaling their luxurious, alien but seductive scent. A few paces away, obscured behind a bead curtain, three people – an elderly man and two women – sit in a small kitchen at a table laid with flowers. They are quietly plucking – not chicken feathers, but flowers: a Spanish still life, by whom? Murillo? The thirty fingers (forefingers and thumbs dyed violet and yellow) appear to work independently of their hands, folding back petals to remove the three stigmas. Kneeling beside the table, I try the plucking, copying their movements, my own clumsy and slow-fingered. The older woman corrects me, and with an elegant staccato flick of the wrist –

as though demonstrating the playing of a castanet – flicks the stigma decisively on to its pile.

A few feet away from the pluckers, perched on top of an old Calor-gas heater, is a garden-sized wire mesh sieve, inside which the brilliance and juice of the stigmas are being 'toasted' away as the flowers turn into spice. This 'toasting' takes about five minutes, reducing the featherweight stigmas by 80 per cent of their weight. (In 1728 the Saffron Walden 'crocers' took twenty-six hours to do their 'toasting'. The result was called hay saffron. When compressed, it was cake saffron.)

Further down the road, on the other side of another bead curtain, is a small, deserted, bottle-less bar. Behind its empty counter, where bartenders would normally stand, are rows of flower pots of flowering *Crocus sativus*. This is where I bought my pot.

That afternoon the competition to judge the saffron pluckers takes place in another courtyard. Behind iron railings, at a trestle table laid with white cloths, about twelve pluckers sit in white plastic armchairs. The courtyard is full of onlookers, expectation and two big policemen whose holsters contain guns. The pluckers – all women of different ages, though predominantly of the grandmother generation, dressed in their Sunday best – sit on one side of the table. In front of each is a transparent plastic bag puffed out with crocus flowers. The saffron compère, a plump youngish man, rushes to and fro making sure that the contestants are correctly numbered. Tension increases. Finally he shouts, 'Silencio!' The chattering audience becomes quiet.

'Uno, dos, TRES!' The competitors empty their bags on to the table and begin separating. The winner will be the fastest and neatest worker.

The audience presses forward, friends and family encouraging. This is the oddest, most endearing of 'races', between sedate, seated countryside women. Dozens (or rather tens) of agile, hard-working fingers and thumbs move this way and that. The audience's eyes rove up and down the table watching the diminishing piles.

At last the first plucker to finish stands up, flushed, smiling and a little embarrassed. The audience applauds. The policemen smoke.

There will probably be semi-finals and demi-semi-finals before the winner is decided – but before then the last bus back to Toledo arrives.

There is something unspoiled about both this competition and the little town in which it is held.

Back in Toledo I place the crocus on a window ledge in the hotel. Each inhalation of air through the window brings the surprisingly strong, deliciously flowery scent of saffron, reminiscent of this town's Moorish past.

Some saffron facts

Saffron

The *Oxford English Dictionary* definition: 'The ultimate source is Arabic *za farān* (adopted unchanged in Turkish, Persian, and Hindi); also Jewish Aramaic *za peranā*). The Arabic word with prefixed def. article, *azza farān*, is represented by Spanish *azafran*, Portuguese *açafrão*; the word without this prefix gives rise to Italian *zafferano*, *zaffrone*, Provençal *safran*, *safrá*, Catalan *safrá*, French *safran*, medieval Latin *safranum*, medieval Greek *ζαφρᾶς*, modern Greek *σαφράνι*, Russian *šafran*. The origin of Arabic *za farān* is unknown. . . The Turkish synonym *çafrān* may however be derived from this adj., and may be the source of some of the European forms. 1.a. An orange-red product consisting of the dried stigmas of *Crocus sativus*.

Crocus sativus, the autumn crocus, is not to be confused with meadow saffron, *Colchicum autumnale*. The cultivated form of *Crocus sativus*, a member of the iris family, is a perennial corm about 1½–2in (4–5cm) in diameter, planted in mid- to late summer, which grows to about 6in (15cm) tall. A corm is a short, fleshy rhizome, or bulb-like subterraneous stem, of a monocotyledonous plant, producing from its upper surface leaves and buds, and from its lower roots; also called a solid bulb. The plant has six to nine narrow leaves and a long narrow, tubular, blue-violet flower of six petals. The lily-shaped flowers are usually picked when open – though in North Wales they are picked when closed. The wild form, similar to the spring crocus, was used, though it is now seldom found.

Gynaecological details: three stamens are attached to the perianth tube. Stamens are the male or fertilizing organs of a flowering plant, consisting of two parts, the anther, which is a double-celled sac containing pollen, and the filament, a slender footstalk supporting the anther. The perianth tube is a structure surrounding, or forming, the outer part of the flower. In the centre of the flower is the pistil, which is a bulbous ovary from which arises a slender yellow stalk called the style. The style is a narrowed prolongation of the ovary, which, when present, supports the stigma at its apex. The style divides into a brilliant orange-red, three-lobed stigma, about 1¼in (3cm) long. The stigma is that part of the pistil in flowering plants which receives pollen in impregnation, either directly on the ovary or at the summit of the style. Propagation is by means of the corms and takes place annually, producing small white, fleshy, onion-shaped progeny. Eventually the old corms shrivel and die. The 'crocers' called the stigma (plural: stigmas or stigmata) 'chives'. The Spanish call them *clavos* (meaning nails, spikes). Are they linked, for the Spanish, to stigmata because of their redness and shape?

> 'The flowers . . . opening into five fair broad leaves, with a stile and small threds in the middle of a saffron colour.'
>
> Samuel Gilbert, *Florists' Vade-Mecum and Gardeners' Almanack*

Probably first cultivated in Asia Minor, saffron was used by all ancient civilizations of the eastern Mediterranean and by the Egyptians and Romans – in food ('I must have Saffron to colour the Warden Pies,' wrote Shakespeare in *A Winter's Tale*), wine, cordials and liquors, and as a dye, a scent and a drug. In the seventh century it reached China with the Mogul invasion and was used as a drug and perfume. In about 960 the Arabs cultivated it in Spain. In the eleventh century saffron arrived in France and Germany; in the fourteenth century it reached England, brought (it is said) by a pilgrim who had hidden a corm in his hollow staff. Others say that it arrived long before, with the Phoenicians, when tin trading with the Cornish. In the twenty-first century saffron is grown in Greece, France, Spain, Morocco, Turkey, Iran, Kashmir and

North Wales (see page 170, G). North Wales is hardly synonymous with Kashmir or Morocco, so *Crocus sativus* must possess one of the most equable of temperaments to flourish in such disparate places. In India saffron is used to treat urinary and digestive problems. It is rich in vitamin B2 and riboflavin. It is also used as a sudorific (promoting or causing sweating). Joseph Pitton de Tournefort's seventeenth-century herbal warns that an overdose may well cause people to die of laughing. Homeopathic physicians still prescribe saffron for the treatment of uncontrollable laughter ('*Crocus sativus*, three every ten minutes'; however, when there is 'laughing at serious things', take phosphorus, three every ten minutes). Is this an example of the homeopathic maxim: *similia similibus curantur* (let like be treated by like)?

In fourteenth-century England saffron was considered a commodity of great commercial value. Anyone found adulterating it suffered severe penalties – even death. In Ancient Greece it was a royal colour; Homer and Hippocrates wrote about it. In Ancient Rome it was used as a scent and a dye. When Nero made his entrance, the streets were sprinkled with saffron – no doubt the flowers, not the spice.

'6,744,320 flowers are required to yield one ounce of saffron.'
Jonathan Pereira (1804–53), *The Elements of Materia Medica*

Saffron calculations – from different sources

70,000 flowers produce 1lb (avoirdupois) (450g) saffron.
20,000 (dried) stigmas produce 4oz (110g) saffron.
4,300 blossoms produce 1oz (25g) dried saffron.

I can't remember from where I got these figures.

Who does the counting?

Saffron is the most expensive spice in the world. It costs ten times as much as vanilla and fifty times as much as cardamom. It is astonishing that something so small and fragile, just a whisker-thin filament that has been toasted and shrivelled, should be filled with such powerful colour, scent and taste.

It is convenient for the consumers of saffron that the aching backs and fingers of the saffron farmers do not make their presence known in the taste of a paella, bouillabaisse or risotto Milanese.

What a pack of thieves we are. We steal the stigma from the saffron flower, the eggs from the sturgeon, the truffle from its oak host, the pearl from the oyster, the oyster from its shell, and the liver from the goose.

The report

Available to eat and observe now are basil, both bush and sweet. *Lilium regale* has already made several seed containers: mullion-windowed, airy, yet enclosed. Garlic chives are plentiful, and so are the thin-leaved chives that look less timid. Aubergine flowers continue to ruminate, uncertain whether to bear fruit, though there are signs of swelling. Swiss chard and perpetual spinach are producing fresh leaves. There's also rocket, a sprig of Virginia stock, which must have muddled up the months, American land cress, Abyssinian mustard, a little dill and some flat-leaved parsley. Beijing bean flowers are becoming smaller and paler, a final fling before dying. Winter purslane is producing minute white flowers, in twos, which rest on the heart-shaped leaves. Beetroot leaves are opening (still nothing happening below ground), plus the Jerusalem artichoke – half an artichoke was planted and nine white-fleshed offspring now lie hidden inside the 9in (23cm) pot.

Yields and returns; time is money, self-sufficiency, value for money, etcetera

There's value and value. The above produce, especially at this time of year, is not produced in trugloads but in snippings, clippings and handfuls. The aim of this form of gardening is not to be a threat or rival to the supermarkets; it is not for the sake of self-sufficiency, either, so there's no need to worry about yields and returns.

Even if a £1.25 packet of cucumber seeds produces only four cucumbers, the pleasure in germinating them, watching and looking after them (and all that this entails with propagators and composts) and then finally eating them is four times four as great, as far as enjoyment and interest are concerned – a high yield, if one has to think of yields and returns, which seem to be of paramount importance these days.

'Marketmore' cucumber growing report

I had never grown cucumbers before, but I will definitely grow them again, at least the cultivar called 'Marketmore'. They are unlike anything found at a greengrocer's. They are dark green and barbed, the barbs spaced neatly and geometrically. Growing this vegetable is almost like growing a plant version of those prehistoric Galapagos Island lizards.

When the potential cucumber first emerges from its soft-petalled yellow flower, it is covered in prickles. It also has sandpapery leaves and a prickly stem. From what foe is it protecting itself? As it grows older, longer and fatter it relaxes, the space between the barbs increases and the barbs themselves become blunter, less aggressive, eventually dropping off. That something so defensive and heavily armed should also be so juicy and sweet is surprising.

These 'Marketmore' cucumbers like to grow vertically up a stick support, which makes them ideal for window-boxes or other containers.

Bean in a glass

As seed-sowing possibilities decrease at this time of year, now is a good time to observe once again the miracle of bean germination – even though it is well past bean-sowing time. But there is another method, in a glass, where the whole process can be seen in even more detail – and close-up through a magnifying glass.

Take a clear, straight-sided glass or glass jar (small Kilner jars are good) and line the inside with blotting paper, as though lining a skirt. Fill with 1in (2.5cm) of water. Between glass and blotting paper (which will now be dampened by the water) slip in a runner bean, scar side up. Don't let it touch the water; the blotting paper will hold it in position. Place it on the proverbial warm, sunny windowsill. Wait and watch, adding a little water each day.

Don't pooh-pooh this experiment as just something to keep bored children busy. Everyone should observe it, at least once in a lifetime.

6 October, 10 a.m. Use either a bought 'Scarlet Emperor' runner bean or one of the offspring of those sown in April. They will be found inside the now-brittle, cinnamon-coloured pods, which are lined with an almost silky protective 'material' – the potential for spring contained within these dry, rattling pods. If ever you need to know how to wrap and pack, look at buds and seeds – they are most ingenious and beautiful, even better than the Swiss and Japanese shop-assistant wrappers. Why is the offspring bean at least twice the size of its diminutive parent? The parent is approximately ½in (1.2cm) wide, the offspring 1in (2.5cm) wide. Will it, as the months proceed, gradually diminish in size and intensify its energies? The colour, too, is different, the parent bean's coat being a coffee colour with black speckling, the offspring's a dark pinky-lavender with black abstract doodlings; both resemble Bakelite to the touch.

7 October, 3.15 p.m. Seed coat (also called the case or testa) is starting to wrinkle.

8 October Bean has increased in size.

11 October, 3.30 p.m. Still no sign of germination. However, between 3.30 p.m. on 11 October and 10 a.m. on 12 October germination began, unobserved. A white, horn-like protuberance appeared at the side of the scar. This is the root, called the radicle. It points towards the base of the jar. If the bean was turned upside down, it would gradually somersault over itself until it was again facing the base of the jar. This is because it is responding to, and being pulled by, gravity (not because it is seeking darkness).

13 October, 9 a.m. Root has doubled in length.

14 October, 9 a.m. Root has trebled in length and is pushing the blotting paper away from the glass.

15 October, 6 a.m. Root still lengthening; also thickening. Small nodules are developing on the upper, thicker part closest to the scar. These are the first hints of root hairs, whose job it is to absorb water and minerals from the soil.

16 October, 7 a.m. Nodules have become more pointed; bean continues to drink and swell.

17 October, 8 a.m. Bean is nearly twice the size it was when put into the jar. Nodules are lengthening and becoming more root-like. Main root is developing a pointed tip. Seed coat showing signs of becoming too small for what is taking place inside it. The slit from where the root emerged is increasing in length.

18 October, 8.45 a.m. Root is now twice the length of the bean. There is nothing fragile or wispy about these root hairs; they look just as determined as the rest of it. Where the seed coat continues to split, something new and green is trying to emerge. This is the shoot, called the plumule.

19 October, 8.30 a.m. Bean is 4½in (11cm) long; root is now 3½in (9cm) long. Splitting of the seed coat continues. The 'something new and green' is also dividing. Longest of the root hairs is now ½in (1.2cm) long.

20 October, 7.45 a.m. From between the 'something-new-and-green divide', a hoop-shaped stem has emerged, half the size of a little fingernail.

20 October, 4.15 p.m. Hoop-shaped stem is forcing itself out from between the 'green divide'. Easy to see that it is an extension of the root. Hoop stem is of a browner green.

21 October, 8.30 a.m. During the night more splitting of the seed coat took place; it looks ready to burst. But more dramatic than this is the emergence, through the 'green divide', of the 'loop' stem, which has started to straighten and at the tip of which are the wrapped-up leaves, still partially buried within the bean. About ¼in (5mm) of leaf is showing.

21 October, 6 p.m. More leaf has pushed its way out.

22 October, 8 a.m. At some time during the past fourteen hours, the stem has straightened; it is now 1½in (4cm) long and the two still closed-together true leaves have squeezed their way out. This whole process is more like a hatching of some determined bird than a germination. Beak-like leaves still flat and two dimensional but, when held against the light, the veins needed for its life as an adult leaf are visible.

22 October, 12 noon Tops of the tips of the leaves ½in (1.2cm) apart.

23 October, 7.30 a.m. Stem is upright, 2in (5cm) tall and peering over the top of the Kilner jar. Distance between leaf top tips ½in (1.2cm). True leaves are no longer 'sealed' together but slightly apart, the veins more pronounced. Seed coat's sheen has disappeared; it is an old, much-too-small coat about to be discarded. Inside it the bean continues to drink water, grow and swell. It is almost 1½in (4cm) long.

24 October, 8 a.m. Stem to tip of leaf is 3½in (9cm) tall. Distance between leaf-top tips is 1in (2.5cm).

25 October, 7.50 a.m. The two inseparable true leaves have started to part. Between them is the first sign of the growing tip, the 'terminal bud'. Seed coat is torn in several places.

26 October, 7.45 a.m. Stem to tip of leaf is 4¼in (11cm) tall. True leaves are moving apart; veining is more pronounced – it reminds me of cabbage-leaf china.

27 October, 7.30 a.m. Tips of two leaves are 2¼in (5.5cm) apart. Stem to leaf tip is 5in (13cm) long. Leaves are opening. I am going on holiday and won't be back until 2 November for the next inspection. What will have happened during this time?

2 November, 7 a.m. A lot. Leaves are now 3in (7.5cm) long and 2½in (6cm) wide. Stem is 11¾in (30cm) tall and from the tip another three-leaved stem has sprouted. Roots are multiplying, lengthening, fanning out in an octopus manner. Seed coat is now more of a casual wrap. Bean is plump and a healthy bright green. Tip of shoot is exploring the air, window frame, light. Perhaps the bean prefers the caretaker's absence to her presence and being constantly spied upon.

4 November, 7.30 a.m. Kilner-jar method of germination is excellent, because the caretaker has both above- and below-ground activities to watch. Now eight leaves. Stem is 21½in (55cm) tall and fully launched. Daily watch will concentrate on original bean and root area. I feel like offering to help the bean out of its coat, which is now dry and crackly. But inside it the 'larder' leaves are fat and feeding the plant. The roots have fanned themselves around the inside of the jar. The main root, from which the rootlets sprout, has turned green, too, the same colour as the bean; it has also thickened.

6 November, 7 a.m. Waving stem grows this way and that, antenna-like, searching for something to cling to: window frame, curtain, lamp – anything vertical. When it begins twining around a support, it will do so in a clockwise direction. Runner beans always twine from left to right. This was noted by an (unfortunately nameless sixteenth-century) engraver in a bean woodcut. It was with some surprise that I saw this; though why should I have been stupid enough to think that sixteenth-century eyes would be less observant than twentieth-century eyes? (Are there any anti-clockwise twining plants? What about Beijing bean? It, too, is a clockwise twiner.) Bean is splitting open, with striated marks on either side. Only the old coat holds it together. Soon it must be properly planted.

11 November As the bean is growing in an artificial environment and still insists on wearing its torn coat, I helped it to discard it, enabling the 'leaves' to open. They are still held together at the base, like the palms of two hands.

12 November, 5 p.m. Seed 'palms' look less youthful; becoming wrinkled and elderly. They have lost weight. This is not surprising as these seed leaves, cotyledons, are the plant's larder for the early stages of its life and by now must be on the bare side.

Setting aside a few minutes of each day to see what is happening during a minute portion of captured time is worth hours spent surfing the Web. It also seems to create more time.

Château wormery

The inauguration of a third wormery has taken place. Not everyone can afford to buy a wormery, but everyone should have the possibility of owning one.

This experimental wormery consists of a 20 x 13 x 7in (50 x 33 x 18cm) wooden box. This particular size was chosen because I was given some old wooden wine boxes (Château Haut-Batailley, 1978) of those dimensions and it seemed right for a little balcony – or anywhere else small. How 'right' the change from wine box to wormery will feel to the friend who gave me the box remains to be seen. Along the top of the long end I drilled about seven holes. Use the biggest bit available – about the size of a little finger. Along the bottom of the long end I drilled another set of holes. I then lined the box with a postman's sack (made of polypropylene). 'Lining' means just laying the sack inside the box so that its base and sides are covered and worm-proof. Sometimes these sacks are left in the street; Post Office sorting offices might not mind selling or giving them away. See page 171, K, for suppliers of these and coir bricks. Coir bricks are made of coconut fibre, which (when water is added) expand into a comfortable, peat-like bedding for the worms. Don't hydrate the coir brick until the worms arrive. Instead of the brick, mature compost or leaf mould can be used. As long as it is moist, loose and not sodden, it will do.

When the château is ready, order the worms (see page 171, K). When they arrive, place the coir brick in a bucket and add water, following the accompanying instructions. The brick will expand and break up. Sift through it to remove any lumps. When the coir becomes a bran-like mash, place it in a layer on the base of the château, smoothing the surface. Make a small, nest-like indentation in the centre of the box and place the worms inside; then cover with a little coir. Protect the surface with a damp newspaper or cardboard – the latter is preferable because it has more air in it. Place the château on a couple of lengths of wood, to allow drainage. Then create a waterproof, but not airproof, cover by cutting a piece of plastic and making an open-sided envelope to wrap loosely over the whole box, leaving the ends open. Secure loosely with a large clip. If possible, shelter the château beneath a table or chair – anything to keep out the rain.

Next day make another nest-indentation in the coir and fill it with a handful of saved-up kitchen-waste food. Cover with more coir and the newspaper or cardboard. Don't disturb the worms. Some wormerers divide their wormeries into neat segments of six or eight (or whatever number you choose) and, depending on how big the wormery is, leave the food in a different segment each time. This is quite a good idea for orderly people, as the worms' appetite can then be checked.

Keep a watch on the coir in case it becomes too dry. If it does, water but don't drench it, remembering how the coir felt when it was first put into the box.

If another type of wormery is being used, now is the time to protect it from the cold with an eiderdown of bubble wrap. Tuck this round the wormery, making sure that air can still enter.

Refreshing the window-boxes

After spending spring and summer squashed inside the window-boxes and pots, soil can become compacted and heavy. Before sowing in late autumn, turn the window-boxes and pots upside down and sift through the soil, removing any roots and lumps and refreshing it for the new occupants. Add a handful of chicken pellets to encourage the seeds on their way.

(I am not certain that the so-called self-watering window-boxes are such a good invention. They have a reservoir at the bottom, which generally remains full, creating self-bog-making window-boxes.)

Potato possibilities

October–November is the time to order seed potatoes for delivery between December and March:

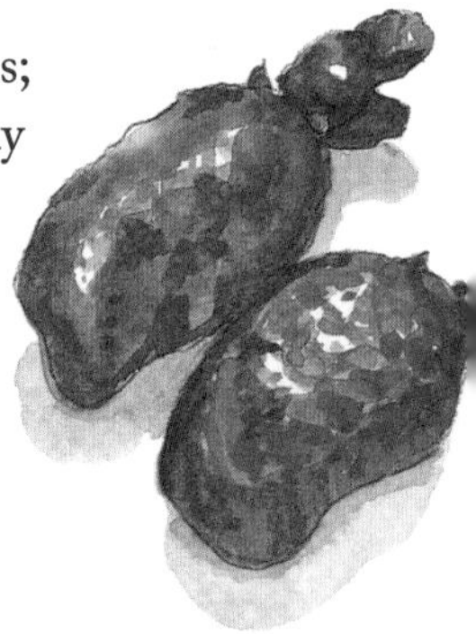

'Blue Kerr's Pink': a blue 'sport' of a pink variety
'Dunluce': early maturing, and good for potato salads; can also be grown in growbags; ready in early May
'Edgcote Purple': an old Northamptonshire potato, also once known as 'Port Wine Kidney', 'Black Kidney' and 'Gloucester Flukes', among other names; a rich, all-over vinous purple
'Etoile du Nord': pink maincrop
'Magnum Bonum': a parent of 'King Edward'; popular with the Victorians
'Purple Congo'
'Salad Blue': blue all the way through, even after it has been cooked
'Salad Red': pinkish flesh, chestnut-ish flavour and texture
'Sefton Wonder': russet skinned and therefore slug resistant
'Shetland Black': it really is black

This list is just a sample; there are dozens more varieties. Choose some, or one, from the 'Museum Collection' of old rare and unusual varieties (see page 171, L).

Some people think that a potato is a potato is a potato. It is not: they are all different in taste, texture, colour, smell and shape, and deserve to be remembered by their different names, not lumped together as 'just potatoes'.

Small suppliers of potatoes are more interesting and patient (they don't mind answering questions) and are often prepared to send just a few samples. At the height of my potato-growing passion,

I had an interesting relationship with the Macleans of Perthshire. Donald Maclean spent years gathering the largest private collection in the world of potato cultivars (a cultivar is a variety that has arisen in cultivation) – a potato library. He once exhibited 367 varieties at the Royal Horticultural Society Halls in London. It was he who rediscovered many forgotten potatoes, including 'Salad Blue'.

Occasionally I would send him a potato brought back from somewhere like Iceland or Egypt. In return he would send me a handful of rare potatoes, packed in an old custard box. These lumpy presents (he and his wife Margaret refused payment) were most enjoyable to receive.

Donald Maclean died in 1988. His wife continued the potato farm until 1995, when she retired and another husband and wife, G.M. and E.A. Innes, took over the collection. They grow over 700 different potatoes.

Unripe fruit and vegetables: don't despair

In 2008 I had the best crop of 'Brown Turkey' figs and 'Gardener's Delight' tomatoes I have ever had. However, 2008 did not produce an equally good summer and by the time autumn arrived the figs and tomatoes were still green, rock hard and more suitable as ammunition than fruit.

In October, while I was searching for recipes for unripe figs and green tomatoes, suddenly, as though a switch had been turned on, they started to relent and ripen. This was strange because there was no noticeable increase in temperature or sunshine. The figs developed maroon markings and began to respond to a gentle squeeze. The tomatoes turned orange. Small slits appeared in the now plump figs making them resemble Mr Pickwick bursting out of his too tight waistcoat. A week later the tomatoes were red and dropped willingly into the palm of one's hand. The fig slits widened, revealing intimate dark pink interiors. Both fruits contained all the stored-up sweetness of summer and autumn. From where does this miraculous sweetness come?

Seeds to sow now, outdoors

(But only for the patient, as they take much longer to germinate at this time of the year. What are they doing deliberating beneath the soil? What tempts them to emerge?)

Lamb's lettuce (*Valerianella locusta*) 'Dante' and 'Suttons' Large Leaved'
Radish (*Raphanus sativus*) 'Red Meat'

As soon as the heating needs to be turned on, the growing of indoor mushrooms can begin (see opposite).

WHAT TO EAT NOW

Jerusalem artichoke salad

This is an unusual, nutty salad.

1 tbsp (15ml) white wine vinegar

5 tbsp (75ml) olive oil

Pinch of mustard

Sea salt and pepper

Jerusalem artichokes, about 1lb (450g) for a trial salad

Prepare the vinaigrette by combining the vinegar, oil, mustard, salt and pepper. Peel the artichokes as thinly as possible. Grate, on a fine grater, into the vinaigrette and mix immediately.

November

From outdoors to indoors

There are seeds that can be sown outdoors now, but as outdoors is no longer tempting – at least for doing slow things like seed sowing – now is the time to do indoor gardening. Before going indoors, there is still some outdoor work to be completed (see page 128). Snap up every sunny opportunity; the sunlight will be golden but lined with ice.

Growing mushrooms

I used to do this quite successfully in the sitting room. This doesn't mean that carpets and rugs were sprouting champignons and fairy rings: the mushrooms were contained in a plastic bucket.

These buckets have now been replaced by polystyrene boxes measuring about 10 x 13 x 6in (25 x 33 x 15cm). There are two (maybe more) types of champignons that can be grown indoors: organic and inorganic. They can be bought or ordered from some (not all) nurseries and garden centres.

Mushroom

The *Oxford English Dictionary* definition: 'Originally: a fleshy fungal fruiting body consisting of a stalk and a dome-shaped cap lined underneath with gills; the macroscopic fruiting body of a fungus, esp. a basidiomycete. Later also: any fungus, esp. an agaric or other basidiomycete. In popular use mushroom has often been reserved for edible species, toadstool being applied to inedible or poisonous ones . . . The mushroom is proverbial for its rapid growth.'

When growing mushrooms you enter a quite different world from that of plants. Plants belong to the plant kingdom. Animals are members of the animal kingdom. Mushrooms and toadstools have their own separate kingdom, the fungus kingdom. The words describing fungi are also different: there are universal veils, vulva, spores, fruiting bodies, fairy rings, mycelium, gills, partial veils, hyphae and many more.

Fungi differ from plants in many ways. They don't have flowers, proper roots or leaves, or anything green about them (i.e. no chlorophyll). They don't have seeds; instead they fruit by scattering their spores. Moulds that grow on damp walls, yeast for baking and brewing, and rusts that attack trees and crops are also fungi. Potato blight – one of the culprits in Ireland's 1840s famine – is also a fungus, as is dry rot. Penicillium, the first antibiotic, grows on bread and overripe fruit. The mushroom (what we eat) is only a small visible part of the whole fungus. It is the fruiting body, the reproductive part. Most of the fungus, the mycelium, is hidden beneath the ground in a Hades-like world, from which it absorbs nourishment from dead or living organic matter.

'Beware of musherons . . . and al other thinges, whiche wyll sone putrifie.'

Sir Thomas Elyot (*c.*1490–1546), *The Castel of Helth*

Mushrooms are strange (one is almost tempted to say creatures), seeming to have one foot (or rather mycelium) in the animal kingdom. They appear without warning, silent and cool. Plants don't emerge with a great clatter and bang, but there is always a hint of their arrival: the upheaval on the earth's surface, the sprouting of green tips, the squeaking of hyacinth leaves unwrapping.

The polystyrene box will usually contain two bags. Inside one will be spawned compost and in the other 'casing', which is a peat (in the case of the inorganic mushrooms) and chalk mixture. All that needs to be done is to cover the spawned compost (which resembles giant, damp All-Bran) with the casing. Follow the somewhat idiosyncratically translated instructions (in the case of the organic mushrooms).

Unfortunately, the organic mushrooms are slightly more difficult to grow than the inorganic, being fussy about the different temperatures in which they need to flourish. A thermometer will be needed. I have several, causing my flat to resemble a cottage hospital: in fact there is one thermometer, and sometimes two, per room – the second to keep an eye on the first.

(Apart from George Bernard Shaw's Hertfordshire house, I know of no other house that contains so many thermometers and barometers. If I knew why Shaw was so interested in the rise and fall of mercury, I might know why I am. Mercury is a magical substance and a broken thermometer is something to look forward to. When the vertical liquid silver, held captive in the thin glass tube, is released, it turns into untouchable, uncatchable, star-coloured globules, infinitely more tempting to taste and feel on the tongue than silver cake decoration balls. But it is lethal.)

The organic mushrooms like to begin the first five to eight days of their life at a temperature of 68–77°F (20–25°C), conveniently the temperature inside the airing cupboard. Then for one day they prefer a temperature of about 59°F (15°C). After this they need to spend the rest of their indoor life, which may be a month or six weeks, at a more temperate 59–64°F (15–18°C). Cohabiting with organic mushrooms can be just as tricky as setting up house with the seedling propagator. If you are too hot or too cold, never mind, just turn on a fan or drink lemon with honey – the seedlings and mushrooms come first or they will die. You, probably, won't.

Autumn and early winter are a good time to grow mushrooms. This is when they grow naturally outdoors.

'For wine we left our heath, and yellow brooms,
And cold mushrooms.'
John Keats (1795–1821), *Endymion*

When the mushroom container has been prepared, you might well wonder what is going on inside this apparently unpromising-looking polystyrene box, normally filled with objects such as radios and video recorders, but now filled with compost and spores. Apart from the faint woody smell, there is no suggestion of what is taking place. Beneath the soil or peat mixture, white-ish cobweb-like threads will begin to radiate out from the invisible spores, creating a constellation. These, the mycelia, are the equivalent of roots. Mycelia may be finer than hair or (in some species) as thick as bootlaces. When underground, they can stretch for many yards – some say miles. The mushrooms eventually die, but the mycelium continues to live. When two threads from two different spores meet, a swelling begins and a mushroom starts to grow.

Before this can happen, two to three weeks must pass; the compost should be kept moist, but not wet. Test it by squeezing a pinch between finger and thumb; if no water appears, water it. Keep the box away from direct sunlight. There is not a lot to be done in the way of mushroom caretaking: just waiting, watering and watching.

In the meantime smell the compost. It has a woodland odour – something never encountered indoors – and is springy and damp. It makes an even more tempting cats' litter than the seed-compost trays.

Work to be done now

Apart from the worms' monthly treat of ground eggshells, an additional bonus can be a thick slice of bread. Dampen it, place in the wormery and wait. After a few days the bread will be growing furry fungi: penicillium. Lift the slice gently; beneath it will be snuggled a little group of worms, using the bread as an edible air-raid shelter.

Leaves need to be removed – especially from the pond. Some gardeners are perpetually sweeping leaves during autumn and winter. Why not wait until the last leaf has fallen and then sweep? As I don't like putting leaves in the rubbish bin to be thrown away, and don't have enough leaves or space to have a leaf-composting bin, I collect them and then soak them in a bucket of water to soften them, before adding to the compost. This may or may not make it easier for the compost to digest them. Time will tell. But at least the softened leaves vary the compost's diet and texture. The soaking water is used as a cold leaf consommé for the plants.

This is garlic-planting month. If you are going to France, buy some garlic: the robust, ruddy Gallic garlic is preferable to the anaemic-looking, neat specimens found in supermarkets. Divide the head into cloves and plant about 6in (15cm) apart, or singly, in not-too-shallow pots – about 8in (20cm) deep at least. Some gardeners place the cloves on top of the soil, just pressing the root end in; others push them into the soil with just the tips showing.

Sometimes it is possible to buy the bantam-egg-sized single-clove Chinese garlic. Try planting this, too. It can't wait to start producing roots.

If you have sown autumn/winter salads, such as lamb's lettuce and winter purslane, they will need protecting by loosely covering with a layer of fleece (available from garden centres). This is a soft, lightweight bridal-veil material bought in rolls. It is made of polypropylene and protects against frost, insects and birds, although light, air and water can penetrate it.

Sowing 'sensitive plant' seeds

Germinating and growing sensitive plant (*Mimosa pudica*) seeds is supposed to be difficult; even the instructions on the packet say so. Growing radishes is supposed to be easy; they are the first seeds given to children to sow. I have never been able to grow radishes properly, at least in window-boxes, but have succeeded with sensitive plants – even to the point where they produce their powder-puff-ish pink flowers.

Sensitive plant seeds resemble a miniature version of buckwheat. They need warmth to germinate (70–75°F or 21–24°C), so bring out the propagator again. To entice the seeds back to life, soak them for twenty minutes in warm (140°F or 60°C) water. They can be sown from late winter to mid-spring – of which this month is not a part, but never mind. The soaked seeds are laid on the compost and then pressed gently down, not covered. Germination may take from three weeks to a month.

I grow sensitive plants for two reasons. First, because of the extraordinary way in which their feather-like leaves react when touched by a finger: they gather themselves together, almost closing, and then the leaf descends, as though on a hinge attached to the main stem –

or as if suffering from sudden depression. (Is this lowering of the leaves the reason why they are also called the humble plant?) When all finger-touching danger has passed, the leaves rise again. However, they do not respond in this emotional manner when touched by breezes or even wind. In the evening the leaf fronds fold themselves together and 'sleep' – in late winter at about 6.45 p.m. In the early morning they open. What, I wonder, is the difference between 'sleep' and being sensitive?

The second reason to grow them is as a proselytizer, to show to people who think that plants are uninteresting and without feeling – just additions to decor. Sensitive plants are the antithesis of the unpleasant, but popular, maintenance-free plants. There is no such thing. All plants are alive and those in captivity need to be looked after by their captors. Only plastic plants are maintenance free and deserve to be so.

Continuation of 'maintenance-free' lecture: MF plants are on a par with the equally inane pursuits of easy reading, easy listening and easy drinking. If you are too feeble to take note of what is being written, played or in a glass, the sensible thing to do is to avoid all three. Then neither intellect nor palate will be in danger of being overtaxed.

The report

Contrary to what one might imagine, quite a few things are taking place in bleak November. The doll-sized aubergines: it is time to harvest them. What, I feel like enquiring of them, are these exotic, southern-belle vegetables doing in mid-winter in a hanging basket on a London roof garden? Lamb's lettuce is slowly germinating. It is interesting to observe this wary germination time – quite different from bursting spring and luxurious summer. Perpetual spinach, rightly named, can still be harvested, and so can Swiss chard. There are also the parsley and chive families – flat and curly-leaved and garlic and fine-leaved respectively. Also young beetroot leaves. A final handful of runner and dwarf French beans can be picked – not exactly an offering one would have presented to Elizabeth David, but not to be scoffed at. Lemon thyme, with its sturdy stalks and tiny, less vulnerable leaves, is still pickable. So are rocket and winter purslane.

In defence of weeds

I feel, absurdly, almost personally affronted when people refer to plants and insects as weeds and pests.

Instead of just pulling up a weed and discarding it, as I used to do, why not wait and see what has chosen to plant itself in one's tubs – or at least wait for it to bloom? All sorts of different unexpected plant 'presents' appear, some for a brief annual visit, others turning out to be perennials.

I am writing this in mid-November. Sitting beside me on the table is a small bouquet of 'weeds' whose charming flowers are ¼in (5mm) in diameter. They have pincushion-shaped, mustard-yellow centres surrounded by five white petals with pinked edges. The bright green leaves appear far too large for the flowers, as though they should belong to a much bigger plant. The stems are furry, creating haloes.

After a time the white petals shrivel while the pincushion becomes plumper, revealing that it is composed of minute tubular stem columns. These, too, also wilt. But to my surprise, my magnifying glass discovered that beneath them a second flowering was taking place of what must be the smallest, white, daisy-like flowers which would only need a couple of millimetres to measure. This busy little plant performs all these activities during the coldest, wettest and windiest of weathers and is called a weed.

Acquiring an antery

An antery, or formicary (for suppliers see page 171), is an ingenious invention. It is the means by which the life of the worker ants – members of one of the most successful of societies – can be observed indoors and at close quarters. The antery's inventor should be awarded a prize. Every child and adult (particularly those suffering from boredom) should have one. It is included in this book because the owners of most flower pots will have encountered an ant or two and now is a good time to observe them.

The antery is 12 x ½ x 8in (30 x 1.2 x 20cm) and consists of two transparent sheets of plastic held together in a frame. Between the sheets is a narrow space, about ¼in (5mm) wide, which is filled with sand mixed with a little compost. This is where the ants live. Attached to the side of the frame, by 16in (40cm) of transparent tubing, is a transparent magnifier box, which acts as a general playroom-cum-dining-room.

Like the wormery, the ant accommodation arrives by post. It is simple to follow the instructions and prepare the new home. The tenant ants will arrive a few days later by letter post (unless you decide to collect your own from a garden, park or field). This double delivery allows time for setting up the antery, for expectation to increase and for another trip to the children's library.

Inside the envelope will be about thirty yellow meadow ants (*Lasius flavus*, one of more than fifty species found in Britain). They will all be worker ants and all, needless to say, female: all worker ants are female. Yellow meadows aren't yellow but brownish. When they are not living in anteries, they live in parks, fields and gardens. They are also called hill ants because they build their nests in molehill-sized (or sometimes much larger) hillocks. Other species that are suitable for anteries are black ants (*Lasius niger*). They run much faster than the yellows and are difficult to catch, but they are very hard workers and build large tunnels, so they make good antery performers. There are also red ants (*Myrmica rubra*). These are larger than the yellows and blacks and have a harmless sting. Occasionally the supplier runs out of ants and a few days pass until the stock is replenished.

Basic ant facts to contemplate while waiting for the post to arrive

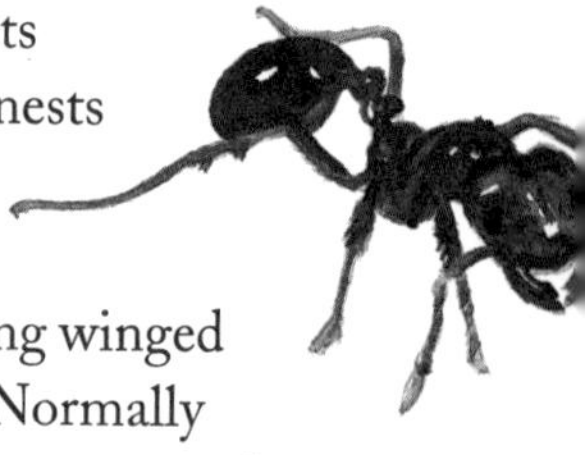

In the beginning: on a warm spring day, young ants – workers, queens and males – come out of their nests and scurry around. Queens are the largest ants, then come the males, followed by the little workers. The young winged queens and young winged males fly off into the sky for their 'nuptial flight'. Normally the queens mate only once in a lifetime with one or more males. After fertilizing the queens, the males die and the young queens then search for a place to build their nests (some will contain two or more queens), where they will stay for the rest of their lives – which may be as long as fifteen years. (In laboratory conditions yellow meadow queens have lived for twenty-five years – sometimes longer.)

When the queen has found a suitable home, she breaks off her wings and digs a small underground tunnel. There she begins to lay her first eggs, which are about 1⁄50in (0.5mm) long. Only queens can lay eggs. She lays two sorts of eggs at two different times of the year: fertilized ones, which hatch into females, and unfertilized ones, which hatch into winged males and queens. While she is on her own she looks after the eggs, cleaning them by licking. She feeds on the reserves provided by the no-longer-used wing muscles – and also on an egg or two.

After a few weeks the eggs hatch into larvae. Inside each larva is a soft body, mouth and miniature jaws. The queen mother (who is also mother superior in this convent community) feeds the larvae. The workers bring water to them. Soon the larvae become too big for their skins and moult. New skins grow.

When the larvae are fully grown (at about 1⁄8–1⁄4in or 3–5mm long) they spin themselves silk cocoons. The cocooned larva then metamorphoses into a pupa before changing into a worker ant. The queen mother helps the worker daughters to break out of their cocoons. When they first emerge they have soft, pale skins. After a short time the paleness darkens, the skin hardens and the daughters begin their lifetime (which may be a season or a year or more) of work.

> 'The success of the ant-community depends on a semi-repression of the workers'
> J.A. Thomson, *Science Old and New*

The girl ants all have different jobs. Some concentrate on repair work; some defend the nest; others search for food for the whole colony. Ants are omnivorous, but one of their favourite foods is the honeydew made by greenfly and woodlice. When the abdomens of these insects (called 'ant cows') are tickled (or 'milked') by the ants' antennae, drops of honeydew are released, which are then drunk. In return for the honeydew drink, the ants protect the insects by driving away their enemies. Sometimes young caterpillars are taken hostage (when they are called 'ant guests') and hauled inside the nest, the captors feeding on the secreted caterpillar juices, while the caterpillars feed on the ants' brood: a good example of a symbiotic relationship. There are also ant millers-cum-bakers. They collect seeds, like wheat, which are taken to storage chamber-granaries. The seeds are crushed and mixed with saliva until they form a paste that is called 'ants' bread'.

The youngest of the ants look after the queen mother, feeding her with regurgitated food. Others wash her with saliva. During this time the queen has been laying more and more eggs – probably thousands. New tunnels are dug and old ones tidied. Some of the daughters are nurses; they feed the larvae and young ants and move the eggs, larvae and cocoons to warmer and drier parts of the nest, supervising the nurseries.

'The lyttelle ant or emote helpeth up his felowe.'
Sir Thomas Elyot (*c.*1490–1546), *The Castel of Helth*

The eggs that the queen mother lays in the summer are different from the first clutch. These are the young winged males and queens. The larvae are bigger and are fed on special food by the nursemaids. When they are ready, the nurses help them to emerge from their cocoons by chewing at them.

The cycle has come full circle.

Something else to do now: root watching

Suspend a hyacinth bulb above water in a glass container (some are made specially for this purpose) and watch the roots 'knitting' until they almost fill the container.

Saffron harvest

Harvesting saffron flowers. In Wales this is done in the early morning; in Spain they were plucking at midday. There are two ways of harvesting the fiery, three-pronged stigmas: either snip them, with nail scissors, leaving the rest of the flower intact. Or cut the whole flower and gently pull the stigma downwards towards the base of the stem, leaving the rest of the flower to put in a pot. I prefer this method because the flowers have a surprisingly strong honey scent – just two can scent a room. They can also be observed in detail at close quarters.

Now place the stigmas on a piece of absorbent paper and then fold it to exclude all light. Put it somewhere warm, like an airing cupboard. After two to three days, or when the stigmas have dried and feel brittle when touched, place them in a small airtight glass jar – preferably tinted to keep out the light. At last they are ready to use.

Seeds to sow now, outdoors

Garlic (*Allum sativum*) cloves
Lamb's lettuce (*Valerianella locusta*)

According to Mr Simpson of Simpson's Seeds (see page 170), the following may also be sown now:

Borecole (*Brassica oleracea* Acephala Group), also called kale or cavolo nero
Broad beans (*Vicia faba*) 'Aquadulce Claudia'
Carrot (*Daucus carota*) 'Amsterdam 3'
Swiss chard (*Beta vulgaris* Cicla Group)
Chinese mustard 'Green in Snow'
Garlic (*Allium sativum*) 'Moraluz' and 'Sprint'
Lettuce (*Lactuca sativa*) and salad leaves 'Rougette de Montpellier' and 'Black Seeded Simpson'
Mangetout (*Pisum sativum*) 'Sugar Dwarf Sweet Green'
Radish (*Raphanus sativus*) 'China Rose'

Potato (*Solanum tuberosum*) planting suggestions: 'International Kidney' (Jersey Royal®)

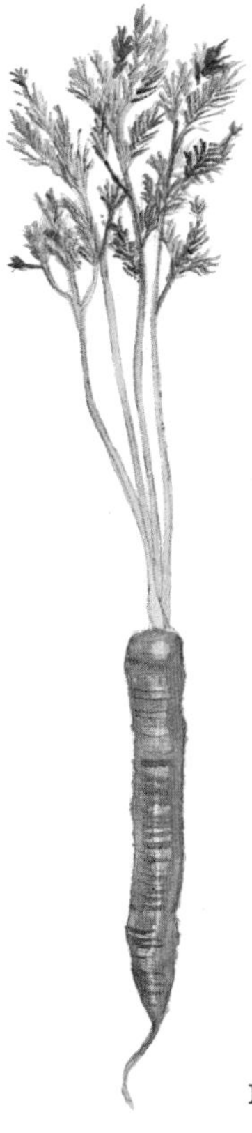

WHAT TO EAT NOW

A simple version of Risotto alla Milanese

Although saffron, like truffles, is not a shy spice, the simpler and fewer the ingredients it is combined with when cooking, the better the results.

pinch of saffron (about 10 filaments)

approximately 1¾ pints (1 litre) organic chicken stock (using a cube if necessary)

1oz (25g) butter

12oz (350g) rice (in order of preference: carnaroli, vialone nano, arborio)

1oz (25g) Parmesan, freshly grated

more Parmesan and butter for serving at the table

Pound the saffron filaments and steep in an eggcupful of stock. Simmer the chicken stock in a small saucepan. Melt the butter in a heavy medium-sized pan. When the butter is melted, add the rice and stir until coated. Add a ladleful of stock to the rice and stir until absorbed. Continue feeding the rice with stock until it can absorb no more and is of a creamy but not sticky consistency. Some rice – depending on the type and when it was harvested – is thirstier than others. When adding the final ladleful of stock, also add the steeped saffron, butter and grated Parmesan. Stir and serve.

December

Nasturtium resurrection

December. The nasturtiums are still scrambling up and down the trellis as brilliantly orange and ebullient as they were at midsummer. The unusual thing about these particular flowers is that they have two flushes, behaving as though they are perennials instead of annuals. The first flush (sown the previous spring) flower when the seeds of the second flush are still in the ground contemplating what to do next. During the previous autumn I will have removed (or think I have removed) all the old tangled growth. But obviously I have not because remnants of the plants will still be hiding in the soil ready to resurrect in the early spring. Their flowers are particularly bright; great scarlet waterfalls of them cascade out of the containers. Their stems and leaves are paler, as though filled with diluted sap, and have an elderly, less vigorous appearance, perhaps exhausted by their unusual perennial existence.

Next year's growing possibilities

December is an appropriate hibernation period in which to contemplate next year's growing possibilities. A good place to do the contemplating is in front of the fire, burning the recycled local newspaper 'logs', while the headlines waft up the chimney, as ephemeral now as they were in print. 'Gardener's Delight' tomatoes, 'Salad Bowl' lettuce, perpetual spinach, Swiss chard and rocket, why not branch out and do something different? The following is a next-year possibility plan: to specialize in sowing different basils and tomatoes – it would be difficult to find better bedfellows. Specializing is rewarding because it enables the gardener to really get to know one plant and all its possibilities, instead of having just a superficial acquaintance. For instance, most people have no idea how many different basils there are. Here is a list taken from just two catalogues (see page 170, C and D).

Basil list

Sweet basil (*Ocimum basilicum*)

Cultivars include:
'Fino Verde': with true sweet basil aroma and taste
'Genovese' (perfume basil): grown in Italy, almost perfumed aroma and flavour
'Green Globe': a refined, compact basil of Italian origin
'Green Ruffles': novelty basil, leaves ruffled and fringed
'Napolitano' (syn. 'Mammoth'): large lettuce leaves with crinkled edges; rich, mellow flavour; grown around Naples
Then there are the purple-leaved sweet basils (*O. b.* var. *purpurascens*), including:
'Dark Opal': strong basil scent and very decorative, with purple leaves and pale pink flowers
'Purple Ruffles': dark purple leaves that are fringed and quilted; pinkish-purple flowers; strong basil scent
'Red Rubin': purple-bronze leaves

Bush basil (*O. minimum*): small leaves, spherical shape Cultivars include:
'Greek': a popular cultivar which, as its name implies, is often grown in Greek homes and restaurants
'Spicy Globe': a form with a dense globular habit; extra-strong spicy flavour and fragrance

Holy basil, sacred ka prao or purple tulsi (*O. tenuiflorum*): believed to be the sacred basil from Thailand grown around Buddhist temples; clove-like scent; used in India for its medicinal properties – said to be very helpful for ailments such as sinus problems and fungal skin infections. Another variant of *O. tenuiflorum* is the Thai Horapha basil, with anise scent and red stems and bracts with pinky-white flowers. Cultivars of Horapha basil include:

'Anise': decorative mulberry-tinted plant with pale pink flowers and anise fragrance

'Liquorice': used in South-East Asian cooking

Citrus and spicy basils (*O.* x *citriodorum*)

Cultivars include:

'Cinnamon' (syn. 'Mexican'): cinnamon-clove aroma, light green leaves with reddish stems

'Lemon': Indonesian kemangie; grey-green leaves and lemon scent; use for tea

'Mrs Burns' (syn. 'Lime'): similar to lemon basil but with a distinct lime flavour; dark green small leaves

'Spice': dark green, slightly hairy leaves, very aromatic; long stems of pink flowers, decorative when dried

Interesting oddities

New Guinea (*O. cambechianum*): purple flowers, purple veins

Tree (*O. gratissimum* = most pleasing): also known as East India or clove basil; fuzzy lime-green leaves (burning leaves are used to repel mosquitoes); small pale yellow flowers; can reach 8ft (2.5m) in height

Lists of different tomatoes are more readily available, though for containers it is preferable to keep to the pot-grown varieties; the others can become too domineering.

Something else worth concentrating on would be unusual potatoes (see list on page 122), not those available in shops. Also dill – from a smaller family than basil, but, when added to potatoes, a perfect combination. (If I could take only two herbs to a desert island, I would choose basil and dill.)

Dill list

Dill (*Anethum graveolens*): used as a herbal remedy to assist digestion
'Dukat': selected for leaf production
'Fernleaf': a unique strain, producing dwarf plants with dark green leaves
'Herkules': a cultivated variety, larger than ordinary dill, and bred for strong flavour
Indian (*Anethum graveolens* var. *sowa*): pungent leaves, used extensively in India and the Far East; seeds used for flatulence
'Mammut': for seed production
'Vierling': extra-strong stems, bluish-green leaves; often used as a cut flower.

Second plan for next year: to plant different fruit. Redcurrants grow well in tubs. So do raspberries, particularly the variety called 'Autumn Bliss' (see page 170, F). Also try a 12in (30cm) tall *Pyrus communis* 'Doyenné du Comice' pear, available from some garden centres.

The ants' arrival

They arrive by post in a small Jiffy bag labelled 'Urgent: Live Creatures'. Inside the bag is the playroom-cum-dining-room (a small, transparent, circular magnifier box with lid). Inside it is a little compost and thirty yellow meadow ants – all female workers with wasp waists. The box has a jutting-out tube capped with a plug; so has the antery.

A 1in (2.5cm) piece of the transparent plastic tubing is cut, the plugs removed and then the travelling box and antery are joined by the snipped-off tubing. Any squeamishness concerning ants seems to disappear when your concentration is focused on the actual yellow meadows rather than the idea of them.

Now comes an interesting moment: the crossing of the Rubicon from travelling box to antery. Three workers approach the tunnel. They must sense that something has happened. They seem to be having a discussion. The bravest stands on her back legs and enters the tunnel, but then quickly scampers back to the others. A few seconds later the lone explorer sets off again. This time she goes right into the antery. Will she discover the two introductory tunnels? (These are made when setting up the antery by inserting a pipette-like instrument (supplied) into the sand to make a couple of matchstick-sized tunnel entrances to remind the new residents about tunnelling and give them encouragement.) In the box, discussion continues between the twenty-nine less brave workers.

About five minutes later a few more yellow meadows venture forth. How long will it take them to find the 'playroom' and the 16in (40cm) long transparent tube tunnel? Not long. They are already racing along it, travelling by tube. Perhaps there will be a traffic jam. Two workers meet, going in different directions. They slow down and introduce their antennae, then continue in opposite directions. (Each colony has its own scent, and so does each ant, which is how they recognize each other. How many different ant scents are there?) Sometimes they turn round in the tunnel, a feat which would be the envy of most London taxi drivers.

The yellow meadows arrived at 9 a.m. By 10.15 a.m. they had all crossed over into the antery, except for two diffident workers. By noon there was only one left in the box. The others had already started tunnelling.

Ants don't need to be fed often: just once a week, which seems very reasonable. They like juicy food, particularly apples, bananas and baby food, but only pinhead-sized portions. They also like a little protein occasionally in the form of a dead insect such as a fly. I never imagined I would be going shopping for yellow meadow ants, but as all four of the above items were missing from my larder, I did a) because they had had a traumatic journey and b) because I wanted to see what the ant manual had said they would do – share the food and feed each other. When a worker discovers food, it leaves a scent trail back to the nest so that its colleagues can follow it.

Post shopping-trip report: pinhead-sized portion of banana placed in 'dining-room' box. So far no sharing of food has taken place; instead a little gorging has been going on, with one ant lying sprawled across the banana mountain in an almost Roman emperor-ish attitude, probably having eaten too much. When the baby food was offered (a rather unpleasant thick custard concoction of organic 'Vegetables with rice and chicken'), one of the ants got stuck in what must have felt like the savoury equivalent of sinking sand. The most successful menu item is apple – but not any sort of apple: 'Gala', not 'Braeburn' (we have the same taste). First one ant discovers it, then another; a great deal of racing up and down the 'motorway' tube takes place. Are they informing each other and/or leaving scent trails? After a quarter of an hour the speck of 'Gala' apple is covered with banqueting ants. As far as pears are concerned, their preference is for 'Comice' and 'Conference' – yet again, we agree. Don't kill with kindness and offer too large a portion of food. I did this once, and the result: ant drowned in 'Comice' pear juice. Ants can die of 'ant indigestion' and if they are given too much food, they spend less time and energy on tunnelling.

Do ants drink? The ant supplier is not certain.

Dead ants (due to overeating?) are removed from the antery and placed at the far end of the tunnel, perhaps en route to the 'playroom'. As far as I can see, there has only been one death, which could of course have been caused by old age. Another reason for having an antery is that it creates concern for an individual ant, for a life – not that one can pretend to have become acquainted with a particular individual, but squashing one without thought would now be out of the question.

For those who are not permitted to keep animals, ants could be the answer. There is always something to watch, and observing a quite different world gives another perspective to our own. For a short time each day you leave your world and enter theirs. For people who live alone, an antery could also be beneficial: having something else on the premises besides oneself to think about is better than the alternative. The same applies when taking care of germinating seedlings. After a week or so, the workers were tunnelling in earnest, rushing up and down the tube with grains of sand, one grain at a time, though they are supposed to be able to lift between ten and twenty times their own weight (the equivalent of a man carrying a car). The result of their tunnelling resembles a rock engraving, or a newly discovered script –

or perhaps an engraved, curved version of the London Underground. When the tunnels are ready the workers play an ant version of 'follow my leader', traipsing one behind the other, at almost equal distances, as up and down and in and out of the tunnels they go. The discarded sand has all been moved to one of the plastic boxes, which is now full. When emptying the box, remember that each grain of sand – how many hundreds in just a pinch? – has been transported by two ant feet.

'The wisdome of Bees, Annts and Spiders'
Sir Thomas Browne (1605–82), *Religio Medici*

Ants don't seem to like getting up early; they are much livelier at 6 p.m. than at 6 a.m. They don't sleep, say the experts, but rest or pause – sometimes singly, but generally in a little gathering of ten or so, a few millimetres apart from each other. Although an antery is a type of nunnery, it is no place for a recluse.

Edible seed sprouting

Another germination activity for the height of winter is edible seed sprouting – a good introduction to seeds and what happens to them when they encounter water, warmth, light and darkness. There are several ways of sprouting seeds: in a jar, on a tray and in various sprouting apparatuses (see page 170, A and D). However, a glass jar large enough for a hand to enter, plus a piece of muslin and an elastic band, works perfectly well.

Seed sprouting is not a new idea. The Indians, Chinese, Aztecs and Navajo have been sprouting for centuries. Some seed sprouting books contain toxicity information, while others don't. The potentially toxic sprouts (when eaten raw) are French haricot, broad beans, azuki beans, lentils, alfalfa, fenugreek, clover and buckwheat. Mung and soya beans are among the least toxic. As long as no more than 1 lb (450g) of raw sprouts are eaten per day (which seems enough for a horse) there should be no problem.

Always buy seed, and grain, that is for human consumption or guaranteed untreated. Seed for sowing is often treated with insecticides or fungicides. If possible buy organic seed-sprouting seed or grain (see page 170, A and D).

All sorts of seeds, nuts, beans and grains can be sprouted, such as:

Azuki beans
Alfalfa seeds (a complete food rich in vitamins A, B, C, E and K, plus minerals and trace elements)
Almonds
Bamboo
Barley
Black-eyed beans
Broccoli
Buckwheat
Burdock
Cabbage
Chickpeas
Chinese cabbage
Chrysanthemum greens
Clover, red
Fenugreek
Kale
Leek
Lentils, green
Lima beans
Maize
Mexican chia
Millet
Mint
Mitsuba
Mung beans
Mustard
Oats
Onion
Peas, green and yellow
Pumpkin seeds
Quinoa
Radish – a good crunchy, fiery alternative to mustard and cress
Rape seed
Rice
Rye
Salad rape
Sesame seeds
Soya beans
Sunflower seeds
Turnip seeds
Watercress
Wheat

And there are more. The nutritional content of seeds, beans, grains and nuts seems to vary, depending on who is describing them. The sellers of bean-sprouting apparatus seem to endow them with more nutrients than those who are not selling them. One seed expert maintains that 'one half cup of almost any sprouted seed provides as much vitamin C as six glasses of orange juice'.

Begin with one of the easiest, mung beans. As most people know what sprouted mung beans look like, they will know roughly what they are aiming for – though will not achieve! This is because Chinese restaurant sprouts (the commercial ones) are grown under pressure.

Another reason to start with mung beans is that their taste and texture are agreeable, unlike some of the extra-healthy seeds, such as alfalfa, whose shoots are thin and almost textureless, resembling leftover pieces of cotton in a sewing box. They taste like the smell of damp cardboard, though obviously this is a matter of opinion.

Sample sproutings: mung beans

Day 1 Sunday is a good day to start because for most people it is less busy. Put a generous tablespoon of beans inside a large glass jar – no more, or the jar will end up with the mung-bean equivalent of rush hour and all the sprouts will be squashed together. Fill with water, shake to clean, then drain in a tea-strainer or sieve. Refill the jar with water. Soak for twenty-four hours.

Day 2 In only twenty-four hours the beans have doubled in size. Cut a piece of muslin so that it fits over the jar's mouth and secure with an elastic band. Drain the water through the muslin, then examine the beans. Their dark olive-green coats have become a lighter green and some are showing signs of splitting at the waist. The rattling maraca noise they made when dried has changed to a more subdued tone. Fill the jar with fresh water and shake, gently, to clean the beans, then drain again. Most seed-sprouting instructions suggest that the jar should be drained at an angle of 45 degrees and left in this position for a few minutes. Why seeds should like being at this angle I don't know, unless it is the best one for removing the last drops of water. Put the jar in a dark place, but not an airing cupboard, which is too hot – under the sink is ideal. Or cover it with a brown paper bag – or anything dark to keep out the light. Repeat the washing, draining and covering each day – morning and evening, if possible.

Day 3 The mungs are almost three times the size of the original bean, plumped out by water; all the rattling has stopped. Some have discarded their green coats altogether to reveal plump, creamy bodies; others have started to sprout a determined little, hooked, rhinoceros-like horn. Indians eat their mung beans as soon as they start to sprout; the Chinese wait until the sprouts are a few inches long.

Day 4 The horn shoots are now ¼in (5mm) long. Most of the green coats have been discarded. The two parts of the seed are clear to see and look as though they might divide.

Day 5 A healthy white sprout, plump creamy body and, even though discarded, a green coat.

Day 6 Shoots are now 1¼in (3cm) long. At the base of the bean two small legs appear to be sprouting.

Day 7 Small, pointed, close-together leaves – resembling hares' ears – have appeared. Eat now, or rather nibble when passing, as this is when the sprouts seem to taste most delectable and crunchy. Taste them at their different sprouting stages to find out which you prefer. Add them to a bowl of simmering soup stock and then eat immediately before they start to cook. Or make them into a salad by simmering briefly, draining, then adding sesame oil, sugar, soy sauce and roasted sesame seeds.

The glass-jar method seems preferable to the trays, mainly because the sprouts look happier, their shoots are whiter, bodies creamier, coats greener. There is no need to go to the trouble of removing the discarded coats; they add more colour, texture and taste, and without the coats the beans can look anaemic and fledgling-ish.

A friend of mine who has always longed to do a little gardening, but lives in a top-floor flat whose windows are window ledge-less, has become a passionate sprouter, her 'garden' now being under the sink, on the draining board and on a plate.

Before converting the kitchen into a seed-sprouting laboratory filled with jars, experiment with a few trial soakings and sproutings of different seeds in little jars, like those in which herbs are sold, to see which you like most.

Alfalfa – considered to be the father of all foods

Day 1 Follow mung instructions.

Day 2 Follow mung instructions.

Day 3 Sprouting has started: the jar is filling with ¼in (5mm) long walking sticks with brown seed-head handles.

Day 4 Sprouts are ½in (1.2cm) long – resemble untidy knitting. Wash, rinse, drain and return them to the dark. May be eaten now or when shoots are a little longer.

Day 5 The mass of brown knitting with white specks has now become a tangled mass of white knitting with brown specs. The shoots are 1in (2.5cm) long and sweeter to taste.

Day 6 Sprouts are 1½in (4cm) long.

Day 7 Minute leaves have sprouted. High time they were eaten.

Almonds

Use unskinned, preferably organic almonds.

Day 1 Follow mung instructions.

Day 2 Almonds have plumped out; they don't sprout, but undergo a metabolic change similar to that of a sprout. The crunch and taste are different, more like a fresh young almond when it is still milky, moist and sweet. Definitely worth soaking them. Eat now.

Wheat

Day 1 Follow mung instructions.

Day 2 Wheat is slightly plumper and softer; looks refreshed. Wash and drain, not forgetting the mysterious 45-degree angle; place in the dark.

Day 3 First sign of sprouting. Looks more complicated than mungs sprouting, as if there might be more than one sprout. Wheat is now soft between the teeth and the divide between the grain more pronounced.

Day 4 Sprouting three tufts – one probably a shoot, the others roots. It is ½in (5mm) long. Don't wait too long before eating or sprouts will become stringy and 'elderly' in taste.

For the impatient sower and reaper: growing indoor scissor salads

Unhulled buckwheat grain and sunflower seeds can be sprouted, sown on soil, covered with more soil and left to come into leaf, when they are snipped with scissors and eaten as salad. They are supposed to be more nutritious than lettuce. Green buckwheat contains rutin, for the treatment of high blood pressure, and lecithin, for regulating cholesterol levels. Sunflower seeds are almost a complete food and, when allowed to grow leaves, have the additional benefit of chlorophyll. Follow the mung bean instructions. As soon as they start to sprout, fill a half-sized seed tray with about ¾in (2cm) of seed compost, making sure it is damp, but not soaking. Cover the compost with the sprouted grains, using a pencil tip to separate them. The seed tray will be packed with sprouting grains with very little space between them. Cover with a thin layer, about ½in (1.2cm) deep, of compost. Mist-spray with water and then place inside the propagator. The use of a propagator for sprouting is not mentioned in any of the seed sprouting books, but it works.

Next day a few sprout tips will have pushed their way up through the compost. Two days later masses of sprouts will be forcing not only their way up, but the top layer of compost too, making it look like an eiderdown about to levitate. Three days later the sprouts burst into leaf. Remove from the propagator and turn the tray clockwise so that backwards-facing stems now face the light. Start trial scissor-snipping. The most spectacular of germinators – more so than buckwheat or even runner beans – is the sunflower seed. It is difficult to imagine that these large, flat seeds in their smart black-and-white-striped coats could cause such an upheaval, and so quickly. The compost rises with the rising shoots, in places leaving the seed tray altogether and becoming vertical, 2in (5cm) away from where it was originally laid to cover the seeds. What is it like for a visiting insect? Being on a big dipper? At first the germination looks more like a hatching of ducklings as the beak-shaped leaves break through the soil – so much so that it would not be too surprising to hear quacking going on inside the propagator.

Growing wheatgrass

Wheatgrass (when made into a juice) is supposed to be good for us. It would take too long to list its benefits. If it was taken regularly, one would end up embarrassingly healthy. The juice is available in health and juice bars where large trays of wheatgrass, resembling lawn samples, can be seen growing. But unless you find it beneficial and are prepared to invest in a juicer (see page 171, O) there is not much point in growing it – unless you are diabetic, as diabetes is one of the complaints that wheatgrass is supposed to help. As one of my cats suffered from diabetes, I grew it, though both cats enjoyed the portable wheatgrass lawn. I don't possess a juicer, yet, and as I'm not accustomed to chewing grass, doubt whether addiction to it would ever become a problem. Its taste is not unpleasant – the sort of taste that foods that should do us good tend to have.

Follow the washing, soaking, draining, sprouting and sowing instructions. When wheatgrass shoots first appear they are white and hedgehog-ish. The next day (still inside the propagator) they will be bright green and upright. On the tips of all their shoots dewdrops (or is it a form of sap?) balance.

If a choice had to be made between growing wheatgrass or sunflower seeds (apart from the medicinal reason mentioned above), I would choose the latter, more untidy sunflower shoots, which grow this way and that, leaning to left and right or momentarily keeling over. They are more appealing and less military in formation than the regimented wheatgrass. Their taste borders on the delicious: sappy stems, bright, light green fleshy leaves – one could be nibbling a very young 'Primo' cabbage. Taste them at different times during their growth.

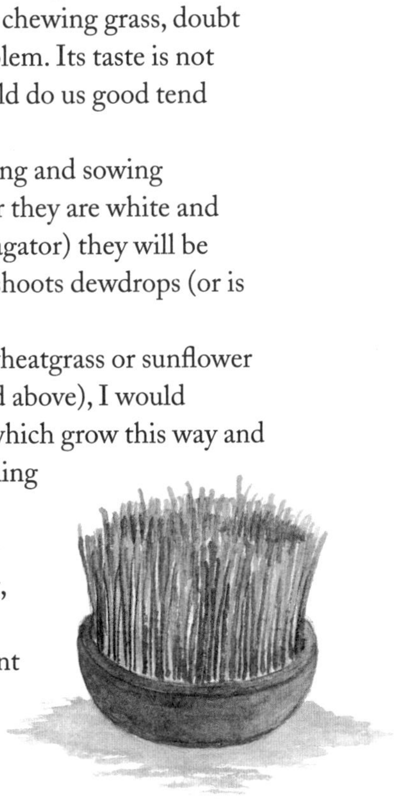

The appearance of the mushrooms

One day, while mist-spraying the mushroom box – which is not unlike a small, well-kept field – there will be the unmistakable smell of mushrooms. A few dots of whiteness, probably at the edge of the box, will be seen in the darkness of the compost. If looked at through a magnifying glass, the dots are rounded and smooth, like minute meringues. From now on the speed at which they grow, especially when one's back is turned, is astonishing: a cap, closed in the morning, will be open by the afternoon. A mushroom can double in size in one day. If one were sufficiently sensible, a whole day would be reserved to watch this drama. The day-old mushroom is covered by the mysterious 'universal veil' (a protective membrane that encloses the young mushroom and gradually breaks down as it expands), stem and cap still joined. As the hours pass, the stem grows taller, the cap becomes wider and the 'universal veil' begins to split as the pressure of upward and outward growth increases, finally revealing both cap and stem.
The fungus has been released but the cap is still closed, gills hidden beneath the 'partial veil'. Only a few hours later the last of the 'partial veil' will part, revealing the gills. The mushroom is ready to release its spores. The ring on its stem, and sometimes a skin-like fragment on the cap, is the remains of the partial veil.

These miniature mushrooms are softer than a baby's head, but cool to the touch – mysteriously cool; the compost has quite another temperature, and so of course does the box. From where does this coolness come?

If, at this stage, you can resist thinning them out by one or more mushrooms, then you must be over-disciplined and will miss a taste, texture and sound when eating that you may not have had before, certainly when eating a mushroom: creamy, dense, noisy when bitten into and, of course, cool and only faintly imbued with the taste of mushroom. The sight of them is equally tempting, their whiteness being of a rich, almost powdery white. To do the 'thinning', gently twist the stem away from the compost; what remains in the compost is the vulva. Cover the missing mushroom space with a little more compost.

Once tasted, it is difficult not to continue thinning whenever passing the box, consuming these savoury sweets with an almost carnivorous appetite. To add heat, liquid or flavouring of any sort would be absurd.

At the beginning, most of the mushrooms grow at the edge of the box – is this their fairy-ring inclination? Then gradually one or two will appear towards the centre. They seem to like companionship, growing close together, so much so that some of them start off as stubby Siamese twins, only separating later on. Their stems are squat and plump, like babies' legs. An insect taking a stroll across the compost might be quite surprised to find itself entering a dense white wood of squat-trunked 'trees'. As more and more mushrooms push up through the compost, crowding each other, they press against the sides of the box, which gives some of them a straight edge.

Value for money lecture number two: whether you have one or more crops or 'flushes' is a matter of luck, and whether the mushrooms are being looked after properly. But at least you have a new word. A 'flush' doesn't only refer to a flight of birds suddenly starting up, the stream from a millwheel, a rush of blood to the face, a glow of light or a hand of cards, but also to a sudden abundance of anything. If there is only one flush it is still worth every penny of your small investment to wait for and see a mushroom grow; then to smell, tend and taste it. There is no point in working out how much mushrooms cost in a supermarket in comparison to the home-grown ones because it is impossible to buy a mushroom with this taste, flavour, texture, colour and 'sound'.

(Spent mushroom compost can be added to pots, window-boxes and tubs.)

Even Elizabeth David frequently mentioned the cost of food. No doubt this was partly because her first books were written just after the Second World War. But why is it that, of all the endless things we buy, food is the one thing we object most to paying for? It seems to be a combination of the puritanical and the parsimonious. Price is not mentioned in the same way when we buy pillows and sandals (though of course they are not bought so frequently), but then most of us don't eat pillows or sandals: they don't become a part of us.

A desktop wormery

A desktop wormery is ideal, particularly at this time of year, for those who, since establishing their outdoor wormeries, have developed something verging on a passionate interest in worms – and for those who have not. I acquired one for two reasons: 1) because worms can be observed at even closer quarters, and 2) because the desktop's worms are earthworms (*Lumbricus terrestris*), which are quite different from the wormery's reds and tigers: a) they are much bigger, b) they eat mostly soil (extracting their food from it) instead of our leftovers, and c) they burrow much deeper.

Although our lives are spent walking, stamping, running, stomping and jogging over the earth, we never – or only occasionally – think of what is happening under our feet. Beneath each acre (0.4 hectares) of grassland an estimated three million earthworms are living – that is approximately 620 worms per square yard (775 worms per square metre). Beneath a football pitch there may be as many as five million worms tunnelling and aerating the soil to allow roots to run and rain to enter instead of just draining away; at the same time they are providing oxygen for themselves. A worm can move about twenty-five times its own weight of soil each year. Charles Darwin estimated that each year earthworms bring between 8 and 10 tonnes of soil to the surface of each acre of land. (That is about 15 tonnes per football pitch – not Darwin's estimation.) But when do we ever have the chance to observe this activity, especially at close quarters? The answer is a desktop wormery (see page 171, K). It is not expensive and makes an interesting present for adults, children and oneself. However, beware: not everyone will be a delighted recipient, or be in the least eager to take even a fleeting glimpse at your latest present to yourself.

Desktops are made of clear plastic and in size are 12 x 1½ x 7½in (30 x 4 x 19cm) and have a lid. They could equally well be used as sample aquariums for travelling salesmen selling narrow fish. Surrounding the sides is a removable cardboard cover to provide darkness and privacy. *Lumbricus terrestris* need little attention in the way of feeding and 'maintenance'; in fact, they almost fall into that unsympathetic category of 'maintenance free', so they are much easier to live with than mushrooms. All the worms need is darkness, coolness, an occasional sprinkle of water and a few potato peelings, grass blades and dead leaves.

The desktop is filled to within an inch (2.5 centimetres) or so of the top with tiger-striped layers of beige and brown sand, vermiculite (provided) and garden soil. It looks rather like one of those dust-gathering sand-sample ornaments bought at seaside towns, which have no meaning when brought home and placed on a mantelpiece. The different-coloured layers make it easy to observe the worms as they glide through them, eventually mixing them up.

Worms can either be bought with the desktop or imported from a garden. My version included six Olympic-sized worms, perfect specimens in peak physical condition, each about 6in (15cm) long and correspondingly plump in diameter. (In Australia there is a giant earthworm which can grow to 9¾ft or 3m in length. In South Africa there is a worm that is the length of three skipping ropes.)

If worms are included, as soon as they arrive remove them gently from their travelling box and place them on top of the soil. Replace the lid. For a few minutes they will lie there, like large pieces of rug-making wool, heads slightly raised, pondering where to go. Then down they glide into the earth and sand layers, only the tips of their tails visible; then they disappear. It is as though they have been lubricated by some invisible ointment – which in a sense they have been, as the 'saddle' (called the clitellum, situated about one-third of the distance between head and tail) produces a mucus that helps worms to slide through the soil. As they enter it a slight eruption of the surface takes place to make room for them. (By how many yards would the earth's surface sink if all the worms and their burrows and tunnels were removed from it?) Replace the cardboard cover, put the wormery in a coolish spot and leave in peace.

How can something so soft, vulnerable and without bones – much softer than one's little finger – glide through earth as though it were blancmange? Try pushing your little finger into soil.

Worms glide through the soil by contracting and then relaxing their longitudinal muscles, which makes them long and thin as they stretch their heads forward, before contracting and pulling in the rear part of their body, which makes them plump and short. They also have tiny hook-like bristles, called setae, which help them to grip the sides of the tunnel and pull them along. *Lumbricus terrestris* can burrow into the earth to a depth of about 6½ft (2m) and in very dry weather they will tunnel even deeper, searching for moisture.

When they have had a few days' rest, remove the cardboard privacy wrapper and they may be seen gliding along, like the most modern of underground trains. The results of their tunnelling – the burrows – can also be seen. These are rounded and smooth, about the diameter of a little finger, comfortable for roots to delve into or even for a miniature White Rabbit to scamper along. *Lumbricus terrestris* is a combination of potholer and miner.

After a couple of days a few offerings may be left on the surface. Potato and carrot peelings, dead leaves or blades of grass – not all at once or it will be difficult to see what has been accepted and what not. Allow one potato peeling per worm and the same with blades of grass. My roof garden is grassless, so grass has to be collected from friends' gardens or parks – I never thought I would be foraging for worms' nocturnal snacks.

When they are in the wild, earthworms leave their burrows and come to the surface at night; they do the same in the desktop wormery when the inspection of offerings takes place. This is also the time when quite a lot of removal work and rearranging goes on. The six evenly laid out potato peelings will probably have been moved to the side of the desktop. Just the tip of one potato peel will be visible above ground, the rest of the trophy having been pulled down into the underworld, where it can begin composting and be eaten in safety. Earthworms have no eyes, ears or noses, so they cannot see, hear or smell. Instead they sense things by the vibrations on the ground, such as raindrops pattering, which causes them to come to the surface, particularly at night. Occasionally they can be observed mating, lying side by side in opposite directions (for mating information see pages 48–9).

Until I bought this desktop wormery, all the things described above had been hidden and unknown to me. Of course there are excellent films on worms, but even though you sit with your face within a few inches of a television, everything is taking place behind a plastic screen. You can't touch a television worm, smell the earth in which it lives or feed it.

My desktop wormery (it is just the right size to fit into a laptop computer's case) has been taken on several outings to friends, without a great deal of success. The first question is, 'Can they get out?' (visits to one's vet are the most rewarding). Desktop wormeries are equally unsuccessful subjects when brought up at dinner parties – if you hope to be invited again. (Compost-making is another subject to avoid.)

Toilet-roll mushrooms

Another mushroom to grow indoors is *Pleurotus ostreatus*, the oyster mushroom, which is grown on toilet rolls. Two white rolls are placed on separate saucers; their centres are filled with boiling water until they are thoroughly moistened, but not sitting in water. They are then left to cool for quarter of an hour, helping to sterilize the paper. The inner cardboard tubes are then removed and the holes in the middle filled with oyster spore, a white, grain-like substance that does not smell of mushrooms and makes the fingers feel silky when touching it. The rolls and saucers are then loosely enclosed in two plastic bags and placed in a dark, warm (71–80°F or 22–27°C) place, such as an airing cupboard. After ten days the centres and tops of the rolls should be growing short, soft white 'fur', rather like that found on the underside of a baby rabbit. The smell of Andrex has been replaced by a faint aroma of mushrooms.

What has happened is that the oyster mycelium has grown through the paper, breaking down the cellulose and using it as a source of energy. The oyster spawn for growing toilet-roll mushrooms (as well as outdoor shiitake, tree oyster and lion's mane mushrooms) is available on the internet (see page 171, P).

After two to four weeks, say the instructions, the rolls should resemble white Stilton cheeses and smell strongly of mushrooms. They do. Now they are moved from their cosy airing-cupboard accommodation and, still in their plastic bags, placed in the refrigerator, at about 39°F (4°C) for two to four days. This drastic change of accommodation should shock them into the fruiting cycle. Is it the equivalent of frost? After a few days they leave the refrigerator and move house yet again, this time to a cool (50–68°F or 10–20°C), light and humid place. Several holes are pierced in the plastic bags at the places where they touch the rolls. At this stage in their life the mushrooms must not dry out. Mist-spray with water every day, moistening the outside of the bags, especially in the pierced hole areas. This will create humidity and encourage fruiting.

Making a spore print

Different mushrooms have different spores, which can be of various shades. The only way to identify some mushrooms is by their spores – as with us and our fingerprints.

Thousands of spores can grow on each gill. Thousands and thousands of spores could fit on a pinhead. Only when the spores are fully grown do they fall to the ground.

Before starting this experiment, examine the underside of a mushroom through a magnifying glass. As far as can be seen, it is sporeless, but miraculous, the fragile gills (similar to a whale's) radiating out from the stem, resting one against the other.

Take a sheet of white and a sheet of black paper and a mushroom (home-grown or bought) – the larger, more adult ones produce more dramatic prints. Overlap the papers, sticking them at the back with Sellotape. Cut the stem end straight across and a little shorter, so that the downward-facing cap rests almost on the paper, half on the white, half on the black. Cover the mushroom with a bowl and leave overnight. Some fungi release their spores quickly, within three hours; others take a whole day or night.

Next morning remove the bowl and lift up the mushroom; beneath it, on the paper, will be its spore print. The markings are so delicate they could have been left by a feather – certainly no engraver would have produced them. The colour? Shades of Burmese cat. The touch of the spores makes even velvet feel rough. All that is needed now is wind or animals: they are the pollinators.

Some mushrooms continue to rain down spores night after night, the prints becoming paler and paler.

Something else to do this month

In addition to visiting the children's library for information, join the Heritage Seed Library (see page 170, B). Reason for joining: 'to help preserve back-garden biodiversity'.

Modern plants are genetically uniform, and that brings with it the risk of epidemics of pests and diseases. Protecting modern uniform varieties from epidemics, and making sure they meet their yield potential, requires the use of potentially harmful chemicals. Planting a diversity of crops, including several varieties, is an insurance policy against disaster and protects the environment. Freedom of choice: why shouldn't we be free to grow the varieties we want, rather than those on a bureaucratic list?

Legislation decrees which varieties may legally be marketed within the European Union. Heritage Seeds are not registered on a national list, so they cannot be offered for sale but may be obtained by joining the Heritage Seed Library. Some of the library seeds were once commercial varieties that seed companies decided they no longer wanted to offer. Then there are the heirloom seeds, passed down from generation to generation. Others are available commercially abroad, but are denied to gardeners in Europe. Garden Organic feels that these seeds are too valuable to lose, which is why it established the library, to make certain that they survive.

So it is not only some species of animals and birds that are endangered but vegetables, too.

Why should all the richness and 'generosity' of the vegetable world be narrowed down to those plants that produce the biggest crops? The seed industry has become the greed industry.

Members of the library can choose six varieties of vegetable each year. The word 'library' does not mean that seeds of the seeds have to be returned, though of course they can be. A report on their success, failure or life from seed to seed might be useful for the library.

The seeds' 'biographies' make them even more interesting. The following will be this year's choice for my window-boxes and tubs:

Achocha (*Cyclanthera pedata*): one of the lost crops of the Incas. Produces fruits 2½–6in (6–15cm) long, akin to small cucumbers with a hooked end. A cross between a minty cucumber and a green pepper. (The achocha may be a bit big for a tub, but you can always try.)

Climbing French beans, 'Cherokee Trail of Tears': the Cherokee nation was forced out of its homeland in the 1830s on a march that became known as the Trail of Tears. They took their most precious possessions with them; this naturally included their seeds, one of which was this bean with smooth, long, pale green pods that have a chameleon-like quality as they mature. The deep rosy blush turns to a warm chocolate and finally purple, with small black seeds that were usually dried for winter use, although the young pods are also tasty.

Lettuce (*Lactuca sativa*) 'Loos Tennis Ball': apparently grown in the 1790s in Thomas Jefferson's garden at Monticello.

Babington leek (*Allium ampeloprasum* var. *babingtonii*): a true leek, but more like a garlic and possibly the wild form of elephant garlic, a different species from both. The green shoots may be cut and eaten like leeks, while the bulbs can be lifted and used in place of garlic.

Sorrel (*Rumex acetosa*): from Russia, where it's called *shchavel*; stays green throughout the year.

Tomato (*Solanum*) 'Estonian Yellow Mini Cherry': the seed was obtained from 'an elderly Russian lady at the covered market outside Tallinn'. Typical of a wild tomato.

Continuation of the toilet-roll mushroom story

After eight to ten (the instructions say, but in my case it was fifteen) days of mist-spraying the toilet rolls in their plastic bags, the rolls begin to start sprouting small, pale brownish-grey protuberances, similar to the velvety horns on very young deer. After five more days and a little assistance in directing the 'horns' to the holes in the bags – or making additional holes where the horns appear – they start growing through the holes, a light velvety grey in colour. The cap heads expand on their elegant stem necks, which lean outwards and upwards from the toilet-roll trunks, like oriental cat-coloured orchids.

And their taste? They have the intensity of a dried Chinese mushroom.

When the last of the oysters has been picked, the rolls are stored in daylight for four weeks at room temperature. During this rest period they should not be touched.

After the four weeks have passed, submerge the rolls, still in their bags, in cold water for eight hours. Then pour away any excess water that has not been absorbed and put them into the refrigerator again (see page 155), following the same procedure as before. This should produce two or three more flushes. If the roll does not fruit the first time, check the moisture level, allow the rolls to rest for a week or two and begin again with the refrigerator treatment.

Horticultural therapy

If, after ant watching, seed sprouting, worm feeding and mushroom growing indoors, you feel in need of some real outdoor gardening, there are plenty of opportunities as a volunteer. It is sad that for some people the words 'voluntary work' seem to have a rather patronizing, Lady Bountiful association. Volunteering is just an opportunity to recycle one's good fortune.

It can take quite a time to find the right voluntary work. I tried a form of amateur counselling, which involved sitting in a dungeon-like room with a red alarm button (connected to the police) at my side and, on the table, between client and listener, a large box of Kleenex tissues. Before being allowed into the dungeon, I had spent two months of three hours a week whizzing at breakneck speed through all the possible problems that might crop up: incest, divorce, death, a mixture of sexualities, suicide and, of course, child abuse. Armed with a teaspoonful of information, I was then let loose on the unsuspecting public. It all seemed not only dangerous but pointless. (Counsellors – waiting in some hangar for disaster to strike and enable them to pounce – seem equally dubious.)

Then I discovered Horticultural Therapy, as it used to be called, now named Thrive (for details see page 171, J), a name that could just as well be used for baby food or an amateur stockbroker.

Here (at the Battersea Park Thrive centre) there are no boxes of Kleenex or red emergency buttons. Instead there are rakes, packets of seeds, a kitchen for preparing salads and drinks, a vegetable garden, a flower garden and an international herb and vegetable bed, and lots more. It is a working garden.

The people who come to Thrive are men and women, young and old, of different nationalities, races, religions and backgrounds. They may have physical or mental problems, or both. You may or may not learn what those problems are. When something is given a label – such as schizophrenia – what does it really mean, to an amateur? You will probably sense more about the person and their problem when sweeping leaves, pricking out seeds or making a salad together than you could from hours of conversation – or, rather, passive listening – across a table.

Ray had a major stroke and was left almost immobile, with no feeling in his left hand. Boiling water felt cold; sharp knives felt blunt. It was while growing 'sensitive plants' that some of the feeling in his hand returned. He noticed that the slightest touching of the plant's leaves made them descend. He also noticed that he could feel these fragile leaves. It is interesting that it was the lightest of touches he could feel, whereas boiling water or the blade of a sharp knife went unnoticed.

Jack, who used to come once a week and whose confidence was at 'rock bottom', would plant something and then spend the rest of the week at home in sheltered housing worrying about the plant, feeling certain that it had died. It was with surprise that the following week he found it hadn't. But then he would remind himself that, if it hadn't died last week, it probably would next. The plant continued to live.

Daisy is young and deaf and cannot speak, except with her hands and smile.

Why is it that the majority of people we work with at Thrive are so thoughtful and grateful, despite their problems? Being there is a good antidote to grumbling. I never imagined that I would be able to work with people suffering from mental and physical disabilities, but quite often it's less complicated than working with people without.

Composting one's identity – yet another way to make compost

I have tried several methods of compost-making, including a plastic sack with pre-punched ventilation holes, a tumbler compost-maker (one of the best but too big for most container gardeners), a bin provided by the council and the Bokashi method (see page 171, K). My favourite, at the moment – though I confess to being a bit fickle about these things – is the last. It is also the most interesting because one can observe more of the different stages in the composting process.

Stage One Begins in the kitchen, where I keep several tin and plastic containers, about 8in (20cm) high x 4in (10cm) in diameter with lids. But anything similar in size will do, depending on how many people the kitchen is feeding. The containers are used for collecting vegetable and fruit peelings and leftovers, coffee grounds, tea leaves, egg shells and dead house flowers. The smaller they are cut, the quicker they will compost. For example, banana skins are cut into four, lemons into four, oranges into six, etcetera. In its initial stage the compost resembles a chunky salad for a large fruitarian mammal. Although it is possible to use leftover meat, fish, poultry, bread and cheese as well as cooked foods, and some people scrape everything off their plates, including bones and gravy, I avoid doing this as I am not fond of rats or mice. Neither creature, the Bokashi instructions assure us, will detect meat and other proteins during the initial composting process, which takes place in an airtight bin indoors. But unless your local rat and mice population suffer from blocked noses, why would they not be able to smell these delicacies when mixed with the soil?

To avoid having my identity stolen, I also add the small slivers of paper torn from envelopes and letters which contain my name, address, bank and credit card details. Why don't you shred it, you ask? Not because I am anxious that the people who spend their nights collecting shredded paper and their days reassembling it will discover my identity but because I quite like this method. Anyway, my shredder only works in reverse 'gear'. I place the paper slivers in a mug of water and soften them before adding them to the bin.

This may sound a somewhat obsessive activity, but I once met an almost distraught man – the patient of a doctor friend – who had had his identity stolen. I have not forgotten him.

The Japanese Bokashi composting method (invented by Professor Higa) consists of two bins measuring 9 x 15 in (23 x 38cm). Each bin has an airtight lid and a sump covered by a perforated base which allows the liquid (the compost equivalent of curds' whey) from the maturing waste to drain into a sump.

Stage Two When the Stage One containers are full, the contents are transferred to the bin. Each layer of waste should be about 1¼–1½in (3–4 cm) deep. On top of it are sprinkled a couple of handfuls of Bokashi bran. Waste and bran are then pressed down with your hands (or a potato masher for those averse to touching things). The lid is replaced, making certain that it is airtight, and the tap is closed. It is important to exclude air to enable the bran to do its work properly.

Bokashi bran, which looks and smells like a tempting, faintly alcoholic breakfast cereal high in roughage, is a 'mixture of bran and molasses that has been inoculated with EMs: Effective Micro-organisms, a carefully controlled mixture of microscopic bacteria, yeasts and fungi that work together to speed-up composting, suppress pathogens, prevent putrefaction and eliminate foul odours'. (I don't find them 'foul'. This is just what people imagine, before they have really smelt them.)

While continuing to fill the bin, remove the juice/whey from the sump. Do this frequently; it does not keep. As it is extremely concentrated, when you use it for feeding plants dilute it with thirty parts of water. Or you can just pour it down the sink, where it will 'help to keep drains and septic tanks clean and free from harmful bacteria'.

When the bin is full, press it down for the last time, cover with the lid and leave for two weeks to ferment. At this stage it resembles and smells like a pickled salad.

Why are so many people nervous of 'smells'? How dull and bland a scentless world would be. The sense of smell must be one of the most sensuous of the five senses. The Bokashi 'whey' has a ruminative odour, what I imagine medieval mead might smell like. Although it is probably not the sort of scent which Dior would rush to patent, it does not deserve to be on the smell blacklist.

Stage Three, waiting During this time continue removing the whey and collecting waste for the second bin. Although the instructions include a list of 'Trouble Shooting' solutions, so far, nothing has gone wrong with my Bokashi composting.

Stage Four, finale I put the Bokashi compost into the perforated heavy-duty plastic sack, mixing it with about twice the amount of soil (it is very potent). I also add cut-up roof-garden waste and exhausted soil from the containers. The sack is tossed and turned as often as possible.

When spring arrives, the top layer of soil is removed from all the containers, this being replaced by the fresh compost. While doing this, one has pleasant reunions with the kernels and stones of fruit and vegetables eaten the previous summer, such as lychee stones, those slow-to-decompose miniature pieces of polished antique furniture. I like the notion that everything revolves round and round, resurrecting, dying and resurrecting. I hope I will do the same.

PS: In defence of snails

'How ingenious an animal is a snail. When it encounters a bad neighbour it takes up its house and moves away.'
Philemon (Athenian poet), Fragment, *c.* 300 BC

If I told you I was going to design a creature whose mobile home it transports sealed to its back, you might be interested. Not only that, this miniature home is also one of the most exquisite pieces of moveable architecture. The domed shell is constructed of gradually diminishing whorls. Imagine St Paul's dome with similar whorls. They probably wouldn't suit it as its design is essentially western and down to earth, whereas the snail's shell has something oriental and voluptuous about it. Unlike the rigid architecture we are accustomed to, snails' shells change in size and shape from the moment they are hatched to when they die. This can take from three to five years. In the first year the shell has about three whorls; when fully grown it will have about five.

Some snails' shells are elongated and appear to be carved or fluted, more like baroque wind instruments than snail accommodation.

Every shell is different not only in shape but in colour and design, too – enough to have kept a whole flock of gastropod[1] artists busy for centuries. It is obviously the different colours and patterns that inspired the snails' intriguing names: Amber, Moss, Slipper, Strawberry, Dusky, Silky, Eccentric, Plaited Door, Cheese, Roman, Mouse Ear and Carthusian.

'As the snail, whose tender horns being hit,
Shrinks backward in his shelly cave.'
William Shakespeare, *Venus and Adonis*, 1592

Snails' shells are not only homes and places to hibernate in, they are also used as air-raid shelters in times of danger. The whole soft body of the snail, called the foot, can glide into the shell. Although it must be somewhat claustrophobic in there, at least it is safe. But this is not the only form of protection. To deter enemies, snails create a whitish, almost transparent bubbly foam – a gastropod version of cappuccino – which emerges from the shell and covers the entrance. If the danger is even more serious, they can seal the entrance with a skin, called an epiphragm. (Some desert snails stay in their shells for years without moving or eating. Not an enviable existence. But they live much longer than garden snails – what a reward.)

'Will you walk a little faster?' said a whiting
to a snail. 'There's a porpoise close behind us,
and he's treading on my tail.'
Lewis Carroll, *Alice's Adventures in Wonderland*, 1865

Another invaluable product of these busy manufacturers is slime. Without slime, snails would remain motionless. Not only does it enable their soft, vulnerable bodies to glide along on rough surfaces and slowly

1 Gastropods, a large class of molluscs which includes snails, slugs, whelks. They have a muscular foot for movement and (in many kinds) a single asymmetrical spiral shell.

toboggan up and down the hills and dales of cabbage patches without the assistance of snow, it also enables them to adhere, even when they are upside down, to branches. Apparently snails can slide over razor blades without being hurt – not a particularly useful occupation, but yet another addition to their CV.

Although snails don't have legs, they make up for this by having four feelers which sprout like antlers from their heads. Two are used for smelling and feeling. At the tip of the other two are two eyes, like lighthouses on stilts. Snails can't see clearly, but they can tell the difference between bright and dim light.

Snails versus slugs

Although slugs are more disliked and are supposed to do more damage than snails, they both seem to be tarred with the same brush. Even small garden centres stock enough snail killer products to turn the whole population into an endangered species. There are pet-safe pellets, snail traps, organic poison, dog-safe poison and, probably the worst, snail tape to which these extraordinary creatures remain stuck and struggling until they die.

A short snail biography

Mating As I mentioned earlier, the hermaphrodite snails' way of mating is luxuriously sensuous and unhurried, the lubricated bodies and feelers entwining and gently touching. They are the complete opposite of those other garden dwellers, ladybirds, whose frantic, unladylike mating resembles two fire engines in a hurry.

Hatching eggs Snails lay their moonlight-white eggs in the ground or in hollows, sometimes producing as many as a hundred eggs. After a few weeks the baby snails hatch, their bodies and shells still soft. At this stage, when they are almost transparent, 'milky white' and about the size of a pea, they spend their time eating. The mouth is under the head and the tongue is covered with minute hard 'teeth' which are used to scrape along leaves and branches.

Breathing They have a breathing hole under their shell about half way down the 'foot'.

Habitat They live in woods, hedges, leaves, grass, flowerpots and dark damp places.

Menu Brown and pungent plants. If not available, green plants, algae or each other.

Activities When it is very hot, or during a very cold winter, they sleep inside their shells, the entrance sealed. Sometimes, like us, groups of snails like to stay close together.

Enemies Shrews, ducks, rats, hedgehogs, large beetles, snail deterrents, birds and us. How alarming it must be to hear a bird's beak tapping on one's shell. Or even worse, having your shell bashed against a stone. Some birds frequently use the same stone for this purpose.

All most of us do to snails is to poison, eat, trap, squash or drown them in alcohol. Seldom do we really look at these intriguing gastropods. Most of the above facts come from a couple of children's books from the local library. For me, they make looking at snails twice as fascinating.

Seeds to sow now, indoors

Italian flat-leaved parsley (*Petroselinum crispum* var. *neapolitanum*)
Sensitive plant (*Mimosa pudica*)
Champignons and oyster mushrooms (*Pleurotus ostreatus*)
Sprouting seeds, beans, nuts and cereals
Lemongrass – find a specimen with a plump, bulbous end; place in water until roots develop; plant outside in spring
Sweet potatoes (*Ipomoea batatas*) and edoes
Root ginger – put in a screwtop jar in the refrigerator and wait until roots appear; plant in a pot

WHAT TO EAT NOW

Pine-nut soup

4oz (110g) pine nuts

1½ pints (850ml) organic chicken or vegetable stock (cubes will do)

¼ pint (150ml) organic Jersey double cream

Liquidize the pine nuts with a small amount of the stock to begin with, gradually adding the rest. Pour the cream into this mixture and heat, but do not boil. If you use stock cubes, salt and pepper will not be needed.

'Nothing satisfies the man who is not satisfied with a little.'
Epicurus (341–271 BC)

Appendix

Seed-sowing, fungus-growing and seed-sprouting diary

The sowing times given are those printed on the back of the seed packets. Obviously where you live – north, south, beside the sea, in a town – will make a difference and you will have to add or subtract months to those suggested.

Seed	**Sowing time/place**
Italian plain-leaved parsley	Any time/indoors
Seed sprouting and scissor salads	Any time/indoors
Greengrocer/supermarket vegetables – root ginger, lemongrass, sweet potatoes	Any time/indoors
'Gardener's Delight' tomatoes	January–March/indoors
Sweet peas (*Lathyrus odoratus*)	January–March/indoors
Garlic chives	February–April/indoors
Sweet basil	February–April/indoors
Bush basil	February–April/indoors
Alpine strawberries	February/indoors
Sensitive plant (*Mimosa pudica*)	February–April/indoors
Busy Lizzie (*Impatiens*)	February–April/indoors
'Slim Jim' aubergine	March/indoors
'Salad Bowl' and 'Red Salad Bowl' lettuce	March–July/outdoors
Perpetual spinach	March–mid-July/outdoors
New Zealand spinach	March–August/outdoors
'Bright Lights' Swiss chard	March–mid-September/outdoors
Baby parsnips	March–mid-June/outdoors
Sweet-scented mignonette	March–May/outdoors
Nasturtiums	March/indoors; April–May/outdoors
Night-scented stock	Mid-March–May/outdoors
Virginia stock	Mid-March–May/outdoors
'Sprite' dwarf French bean	April/indoors; mid-May/outdoors
'Scarlet Emperor' runner bean	April/indoors; May–June/outdoors
American land cress (Belle Isle, winter, upland cress)	Early April or August/outdoors
'Simpson's Sweet Success' and 'Petita' F_1 cucumbers	April /indoors
Annual dill 'Bouquet'	April/indoors; May/outdoors
Komatsuna (mustard spinach)	April–September/outdoors
'Black Seeded Simpson' lettuce	April/outdoors
Potatoes	April (plant on Good Friday)
Rocket (arugula, Italian cress)	April–mid-July/outdoors
Oriental saladini	April–June/outdoors
Vegetable amaranth	April–June/outdoors

Seed	**Sowing time/place**
Iceland Giant Group poppy	April–early June/outdoors
Baby kohl rabi	April–mid-August/outdoors
Abyssinian mustard (Texsel greens)	May–September/outdoors
'Detroit 2-Tardel' beetroot	May–July/outdoors
'Catalogna' lettuce	May–June/outdoors
Mizuna (Japanese greens, potherb mustard)	May–August outdoors; September–April/indoors
Mitsuba (Japanese parsley)	May or August/outdoors
Chicory 'Sugar Loaf'	June–July/outdoors
'Canton Dwarf', 'Joi Choi' F_1 pak choi	June–August/outdoors
'Cornet de Bordeaux' scarole	June–July/outdoors
Saffron (*Crocus sativus*)	June–August/outdoors
'Tah Tsai' Chinese cabbage	July/outdoors
Winter purslane (miners' lettuce, Indian lettuce, claytonia)	July–August/outdoors
Lamb's lettuce (corn salad mâche)	Mid-August–October/outdoors
Radish 'Red Meat'	August–October/outdoors
'Dante' corn salad	September–April/outdoors
Champignons and toilet-roll oyster mushrooms	October–April (as soon as the heating is turned on) indoors
Garlic	November (plant cloves) outdoors
Order seeds	December

Stockists and suppliers

A. Chase Organics
Riverdene Business Park
Molesey Road
Hersham
Surrey KT12 4RG
Tel: 01932 253666
Fax: 01932 252777
www.chaseorganics.co.uk
(for organic seeds, wooden wormeries, Pot Maker, seaweed extract, Organic Gardening Catalogue, organic seed-sprouting grains)

B. Garden Organic
(formerly Henry Doubleday Research Association)
Ryton Organic Gardens
National Centre for Organic Gardening
Ryton-on-Dunsmore
Coventry CV8 3LG
Tel: 02476 303517
www.gardenorganic.org.uk
(for wooden wormeries, Heritage Seed Library)

C. Simpsons Seeds
The Walled Garden Nursery
Horningsham
Warminster BA127NQ
Tel: 01985 845004
www.simpsonsseeds.co.uk

D. Suffolk Herbs
Monks Farm
Coggeshall Road
Kelvedon
Essex C05 9PG
Tel: 01376 572456
Fax: 01376 571189
www.suffolkherbs.com
(for organic seeds, organic seed-sprouting grains)

E. Recycle Works Ltd
Unit 1, Bee Mill
Ribchester
PR3 3XJ
Tel: 01254 820088
www.recycleworks.co.uk
(for Tiger Worm Compost Bin, worms)

F. Ken Muir
Honeypot Farm
Rectory Road
Weeley Heath
Clacton-on-Sea
Essex C016 9BJ
Tel: 01255 830181
Fax: 01255 831534
www.kenmuir.co.uk
(for self-fertile fruit trees, 'Autumn Bliss' raspberries, etc.)

G. Caroline Ridden
Caerestyn Farm
Rhyddyn Hill
Caergwrle
Near Wrexham
Wales LL12 9EF
(for saffron crocus corms, send a sae for factsheet)

H. Suttons Seeds & Plants
Woodview Road
Paignton
Devon TQ4 7NG
Tel: 0844 922 2899
www.suttons.co.uk
(also for saffron crocus corms)

I. Natural Collection
16 Princes Park
Team Valley Trading Estate
Gateshead
Tyne and Wear
NE11 0NF

www.naturalcollection.com
Tel: 0845 367 7001
(for Log Maker)
Also available from Amazon.co.uk

J. Thrive (formerly Horticultural Therapy)
The Geoffrey Udall Centre
Beech Hill
Reading
Berkshire RG7 2AT
Tel: 0118 988 5688
Fax: 0118 988 5677
www.thrive.org.uk
(Battersea Park Thrive centre:
Tel: 020 7720 2212)

K. Wiggly Wrigglers Limited
Lower Blakemere Farm
Herefordshire HR2 9PX
Freephone: 0800 216990
www.wigglywigglers.co.uk
(for polypropylene sacks, Can-0-Worms wormery, worms, desktop Worm World, Bokashi composter)

L. G.M. & E.A Innes
Oldtown
Brownhills
Newmachar
Aberdeenshire AB21 7PR
Tel: 01651 862333
(for a large selection of potatoes)

M. Interplay UK Limited
Unit D, Meter House
Fieldhouse Lane
Marlow
Buckinghamshire SL7 3HL
Tel: 01628 488944
Fax: 01628 476700
www.interplayuk.com
(for anteries, desktop wormeries)

N. Chiltern Seeds
Bortree Stile
Ulverston
Cumbria LA12 7PB
Tel: 01229 581137
www.chilternseeds.co.uk
(for a large selection of basil seeds)

O. Planet Organic
42 Westbourne Grove
London W2 5SH
Tel: 020 7221 1345
www.planetorganic.com
(for hand-turned and electric juicers)

P. Amazon.co.uk
(for organic mushroom growing kits)

Index

Page numbers in *italics* refer to illustrations.